OUR RACE

THE UNTOLD STORY OF AN ALL-TIME SPORTING SHOCK

JASON GARDENER DARREN CAMPBELL
MARLON DEVONISH MARK LEWIS-FRANCIS

with
TRYSTAN BEVAN
with
BEN MERCER

OUTLIER PRESS

1

2004 OLYMPIC GAMES ATHENS
10 MINUTES TO GO

The fastest men in the world stood in single file, the four of them waiting to show the world just how quickly a human could move.

The Athens air was tense with moisture and noise, the teams cramped in a small tunnel waiting to enter the arena. They whooped and called out the other teams, daring them to respond. They had won everything on offer individually so far at this games and now they were going to assert their dominance as a team. No one could touch them. If you did, all you would feel was tight, corded muscle and the iron self-belief of champions, straining beneath their red, white and blue vests.

They were Shawn Crawford, Justin Gatlin, Coby Miller and Maurice Greene. The fastest men in the world.

Prior to 2004, the United States of America's men's sprint relay team had been involved in a total of eighteen men's sprint final relays held at the Olympic Games going back to as far as 1920, winning gold in fifteen of them. They were utterly dominant. The event had not only become an exhibition of a track and field dynasty, but a final-event celebration of supremacy for Team USA. Winning was not only expected, it was expected to be fun. It was expected to be easy. It was their birthright.

Who were these unapproachable athletes, these men that no-one in the world could keep up with? They were sprint deities, picking up the mantles of men on the Mount Rushmore of sprinting. When your forebears belong in the sporting pantheon, figures like Carl Lewis and Jesse Owens, you arrive with a sense of destiny, a belief and entitlement to one day be spoken about in that company. To become a modern day myth.

Their lead out runner Shaun Crawford had recently become the first man in history to break 10 seconds for the 100m and 20 seconds for the 200m on the same day at an event in Pretoria, South Africa. Crowned Olympic 200m champion a few days earlier and finishing fourth in the 100m, Crawford had run sub-10 and sub-20 once again, albeit on seperate days. V-shaped, looking every inch the superhero, he ran with an implacable expression on his face, fully expecting to beat whoever opposed him, whether those were the rivals he beat to Olympic gold or the zebra he'd raced in a television special a few years earlier.

Justin Gatlin was the in-form athlete in the world. Crawford would pass the baton to a man who was not only the newly-crowned Olympic 100m champion but also a bronze medalist in the 200m. Gatlin would go on to be a five-time Olympic medallist, the fifth fastest of all time over 100 metres, a renowned drugs cheat and the man who ended the reign of

Usain Bolt. Then at 6'1 and 23 years old, he had the world at his feet.

Gatlin would be taking the baton down the back straight and handing it to Coby Miller. Miller had recently written himself into the record books as the first ever American athlete to run sub-10 for the 100m in the USA Olympic trials and *fail* to qualify due to the standard of his contemporaries. He was the best of the rest for the Americans but would have strolled into any other nation's sprint team. He was in Athens with a point to prove.

Lying in wait on the last leg was Maurice Greene. The Kansas Cannonball was at 30 years of age the elder statesman of the quartet but in an alpha male lineup, he was still at the head of the pack. A 4-time Olympic medallist and 5-time world champion, he'd already equalled the records of two of America's greatest in Carl Lewis and Michael Johnson, his place on the mountain assured. Greene had been the fastest of all time, holding the 100m world record between 1999 and 2002, and despite all this, had his own point to prove. At these games, he'd been disappointed with his 100m bronze after losing out to team-mate Gatlin and was looking to supplant Team USA's all time greats with another Olympic gold. A man who had nothing to prove to anyone felt like he did.

Even those who didn't make the cut were a frightening prospect. Sydney 100m gold medallist Tim Montgomery, future world championship gold medallist Tyson Gay and Bernard Williams, a relay gold medallist in 2000 in Sydney and claiming 200m silver in Athens. The list went on but they weren't even here. This was the strength in depth of Team USA. How could anyone else hope to compete?

2

2 HOURS TO GO

The Men's 4 x 100m final was set for late evening. For Great Britain, the day had been broken up by a few naps and some gentle walking around the Olympic Village. After a late lunch, they had a meeting before the final relay practice.

There were two warm up tracks in Athens, one slightly above the other. Britain were there early and went for the higher track. The Americans were surprised to turn up and find the British team occupying the higher ground and were further surprised that there was no frivolity between them. They were accustomed to Darren Campbell in particular giving them some stick but even he blanked the Americans completely. Britain were operating on their own, preparing for battle, impervious to any attempted distractions. Feeling relaxed and well-drilled, everyone knew their roles. Despite them being ranked only 15th in the world, they felt as if it was going to be their night.

It was quiet on the higher track, warm in the setting sun and Mark Lewis-Francis felt a sense of comfort, like something was hugging them. They did their warm up lap together, completed their drills and skills and then began to rehearse passing the baton. Britain's theme in their warm up was about projecting calmness and focussing on clean baton changes.

The team's strategy for the Olympic final was no different to the one they would have used at their first ever relay race as juniors. The simple approach was for clean exchanges, to put the Americans under pressure and force them to make a mistake. The Americans would expect Great Britain to wilt, to fall behind, to give up ground or even to make a catastrophic error. If they could just be a constant presence, if they could refuse to go away, the USA might just make their own mistake. After a minimal amount of rehearsal, coach Steve Perks said, "that's enough."

He knew they were ready.

Marlon Devonish was quietly confident. Having seen countless athletes borne on a tide of rising self-confidence have their dreams crushed, he had learned not to pay too much attention to pre-race appearances. Nevertheless, he liked what he saw in his teammates. Jason Gardener, Mark Lewis-Francis and Darren Campbell had not achieved their goals in their individual events and their efforts had been slated by the press. They could have been disheartened but Marlon saw them smiling but determined, relaxed yet focussed.

As the British team collected their things to leave the warmup track, picking up water bottles and tracksuit tops, an uproar came from the track below. It was the Americans. They were heading to the stadium full of exuberance, alerting all and sundry to their presence. The British four slowly, quietly, made their final preparations and were the last team to head to the stadium. It was about a mile's walk away, a long distance for 100m sprinters. Mark was getting increasingly nervous as the stadium was approaching. The fizz from the arena was palpable, energy and electricity from the crowd reverberating out into the Greek night sky.

"You alright kid?" Darren asked him, sensing his nerves. Putting his hand on Mark's shoulder, Darren told him softly, "We are going to win".

Mark had a tingle in his stomach. As they got close to the tunnel, he assumed the persona of his role in the team, that of the indomitable last leg hero. He was the boy from Smethwick who would stand alone for minutes on end next to the quickest men on earth and not be intimidated. More than that, he would need to turn the tables on them and become someone to fear in his own right.

8 MINUTES TO GO

The final few strides from the tunnel into the arena let them know they were at the finals of the Olympic games. The Nigerian team became very loud, the Americans increasingly aggressive and intimidating. The Americans shouted at the British team to look at them but received no response. A thick layer of testosterone, a mess of languages and dialects, thigh slapping and staring in the tunnel gave way to a wall of noise and a sticky humidity on the track. The British team, about to separate to their start positions, gave each other a hand slap and a hug, ready to walk to their marks when that very moment, "God Save the Queen" reverberated around the stadium. Kelly Holmes had just won gold in the women's 1500m. The resulting national anthem gave the team an extra boost. Finally, with chaos all around them and with determination in each other's eyes, Darren called them together to pray.

3

5 YEARS TO GO
1999 WORLD ATHLETICS CHAMPIONSHIPS
SEVILLE
Men's 4x100m Final

The world's fastest man Maurice Greene was pumping his arms furiously, clutching the blue metal baton in his left hand, gaze locked on the end of the track, expecting Dwain Chambers immediately to his left to fade from view.

He didn't.

Chambers had got away quickly for the final leg, matching the American stride for stride. This was not the procession Greene had been expecting. The days of running an exhibition race and receiving a World Championship gold medal for it had gone. The deafening roar of the crowd, the celebratory atmosphere, even the occasion itself, it all evaporated into the sky for Greene and Chambers. There was only each other. Chaser and the chased. Greene nosed ahead but Chambers was right there breathing down his neck as they tore down the home straight, batons in hand. Chambers, eager and energetic, smelled American blood. The undisputed kings of the event suddenly had pretenders to their throne, forcing them to dig deeper than they were accustomed to. With each passing stride, each slap of spike against track and each explosive thrust forward, the USA and GB battled against the rapidly approaching finish line to assert their superiority. This had ceased to be a race. This was a muscular, vein-popping battle for dominance.

Greene had to be the world's fastest man running the perfect leg to win it. He managed to stretch away from Chambers in the closing strides to win it for the USA, emotion betraying his thoughts as he crossed the line, finger pointing to the sky in aggressive celebration, his face contorted in a roar of relief. Greene and his American team-mates hugged and leapt in delight. Violently throwing his arms to his side and facing the crowd in a delighted fury, Greene revelled in the moment while Jon Drummond tore off his vest and flexed his muscular torso to the American fans with hostility etched on his face. The Americans weren't just celebrating. They were lost in ecstasy.

> "A brilliant British quartet performance."
>
> — David Coleman, commentating

For years, the USA winning gold was the default setting at most major athletics championships in the Men's 4 x 100m race. The Americans were the dominant force, full of the confident swagger that comes from having the very fastest men in the world lining up on the same team. Yet on this occasion, the elation on Maurice Greene's face while crossing the finish line and the exuberant celebrations of the Americans in winning were significant. It betrayed their instincts. The Americans were expected to win this event as a matter of course but having been forced to dig deep, their collective body language provided confirmation of one thing.

They were relieved to win.

The British team were now enough of a threat to squeeze every last ounce of effort out of the Americans.

> "Because the Americans travelled to Europe for the Golden League meets, they would know of my European Championship gold and of Jason and Dwain running 'sub-ten'. We were definitely on their radar as early as '99."
>
> — Darren Campbell

The climb to achieving respectability had been slow and steady for the Great Britain and Northern Ireland men's 4 x 100m relay team. A generation of sprinters that had brought glory and respect to British Athletics had retired, with a crop of exciting new faces ready and willing to take their place. World and Olympic Champions and major championships finalists such as Linford Christie, John Regis, Sally Gunnell, Daley Thompson and Jonathan Edwards had been replaced by Denise Lewis, Jason Gardener, Darren Campbell, Marlon Devonish, Dwain Chambers, and many more. The four male sprinters were creating waves within their sport. They gradually asserted their presence on the world athletics scene and were positioned to stand on the shoulders of yesterday's giants.

They made up a powerhouse British relay team at the 1999 Seville World Championships, proving their credentials at a highly successful European Championship the previous year in Hungary by winning gold, with Campbell claiming individual gold in the 100m. At the 1999 Seville World Championships, they were primed to dazzle as a high-performing relay team.

Days earlier, Chambers had taken 100m individual bronze with an impressive performance, lending credence to his rapidly rising profile in world athletics. Jason Gardener had run 9.98 seconds earlier that summer and had also reached the World 100m final alongside Chambers. Meanwhile Devonish, as well as qualifying for major championship finals, was gaining a reputation as a potent weapon in the relay having figured in the European and Commonwealth Games winning squads a year previously. The component parts of a strong team were being fused together and the future looked incredibly bright. Excitingly for GB supporters and administrators, they were all young men in their early-to-mid-twenties with their best years ahead of them. Should they maintain their standards and push each other to improve still further, the future of British men's sprinting was secure.

The Americans could choose from their customary broad selection of superlative athletes to enhance their relay quartet. Their resource and numbers-rich college system had a habit of delivering previously unknown athletes onto world podiums at a regular clip. Often there was no development or strategy needed in order for the USA team to reveal the next sprinting star; it was merely a question of choosing the next sub-ten-second sprinter from an incredibly deep and wide pool for the team. Frustratingly for American individual athletes, getting on to the USA team was often tougher than medalling at many games. Athletes would figure highly on podiums one year but struggle to break into the American top ten the following season. In Seville, the World and Olympic medallist Tim Montgomery and the world's fastest man Maurice Greene were on their team, also boasting the blisteringly fast start of Jon Drummond on the first leg. Any team of this strength but especially an American team, would be assured of winning gold in the men's sprint relay event. That was just what happened.

But there was a subscript. The Americans were acutely aware of the four young men from across the Atlantic Ocean who had been quietly raising their own profiles since the last Olympic Games in Atlanta. Three of them - Devonish, Campbell and Chambers - had been in the bronze-winning squad at the most recent World Championships in 1997 while the fourth, recently crowned British 100m champion Gardener, had raised eyebrows with his sub-10 second performance at Lausanne. Even in these pre-internet days, word had got around. A ripple on a track in Switzerland had caused waves Stateside.

The Men's 4 x 100m final was a nervous, gripping affair. Gardener held Drummond stride for stride on the opening leg, Campbell matched Montgomery on the long back straight, and when Devonish stormed around the final bend to hand the baton to Chambers the red white and blue vests of both GB and USA were so close as to be almost indistinguishable.

Most American athletes receiving a baton on the final leg of a relay during the previous decade and a half would usually at this point be looking at one of two things as they accelerated down the track to glory. They would either be admiring the win in real-time on the stadium screen in front of them or glancing at the clock to check for any potential world records. This time, Maurice Greene could afford neither of these luxuries. The joys his predecessors enjoyed for years had been denied him by a new crop of young, fearless Englishmen. In Seville, Britain won the silver medal, clocking a new European record of 37.73 seconds in the process. They were within three-tenths of a second of what was then the world record in finishing second. It was by any stretch of the imagination, a fantastic performance.

What was more important than the performance, however, was the message that it conveyed. The Olympic Games were around the corner in Sydney, Australia, and Great Britain were now a force to be reckoned with in the sprint relay.

And the Americans knew it.

4

Mark Lewis-Francis was born on the outskirts of Birmingham in Smethwick, West Midlands. He grew up in a single-parent household on an estate in a deprived area. His friends and peers from this area tended to follow one of two paths in life – being led in front of parole boards or by pallbearers. Even as a young boy, Mark knew that he wanted to carve his own path. Despite the family never having much, he knew how to make the most of it, never feeling like he was missing anything. He was full of uncontrollable energy, found it hard to focus in class and got himself excluded from two schools. Choosing the path was easier than walking it for young Mark.

Two bits of serendipity directed him on to a road from which he would never deviate. He was lucky to have one of his teachers, Mr Gibbons, introduce him to sport at school and give him an outlet for his unbridled energy. Secondly, while staying with his father during one of his exclusions, they drove past a large building on the outskirts of Perry Barr.

"What's that Dad?" he asked.

"That's Alexander Stadium, Mark"

4 YEARS TO GO
BIRMINGHAM

The stands at the Alexander Stadium were filling up with fans on the 12th of July 2000. It was a hot day, the smell of burning rubber combining with that of the freshly cut sand from the infield. The large brick auditorium that had taken Mark Lewis-Francis's eye some six years prior was the chosen venue for the trials for that year's Olympic Games, to be held in Sydney, Australia. Along with Don Valley Stadium in Sheffield, Meadowbank in Edinburgh and Crystal Palace in London, Alexander Stadium was one of the primary stadia for athletics in the UK.

British athletics was in rude health. Local girl Denise Lewis from Birchfield Harriers was heavily tipped to win gold at the upcoming Sydney Olympic Games and there was a large, high quality field competing to take the mantle of British sprinting from the great, recently retired Linford Christie. Men's World and Olympic 100m champion Christie had left a daunting standard for the following generation to surpass. Whatever their collective achievements, they would inevitably be measured and judged against a threshold of success that British sprinting had not experienced for decades. The new wave included Dwain Chambers, Christian Malcolm, Marlon Devonish, Darren Campbell, Mark Lewis-Francis, Colin Jackson, Jason Gardener, and Jamie Baulch. These were all names that were quickly becoming familiar both inside and outside track and field and the interest in these trials was unprecedented. Some famous names were going to be left very disappointed indeed at the end of these two days.

Fortunately for those athletes in the shorter sprint events of 100m and 200m, the selectors and administrators at British Athletics had given them a bit of a safety net. If they were unable to finish within the qualification places for their own individual events at the Olympic Games, there was the prospect of being selected for the relay races. This was not new insofar as having extra places for runners because individual events took two, sometimes three athletes to each large event like an Olympics or World Championship, but relay teams usually took six athletes, four for the race and two reserves. This time there was a significantly higher chance of getting in the mix.

Due to these Games being on the other side of the world, a decision had been made to take a larger sprinting team for these relays. The rationale was a sound one; in the not unlikely event that someone got injured there would be a trained and properly prepared replacement on hand. This felt like a sound idea and despite the extra costs incurred, was a win for the athlete as well as the governing body. The athletes were informed prior to the Birmingham trials of the simple qualification process – those finishing in the top placings at the Olympic Trials would be chosen for the relay. This seemed fair.

Yet on the day of the trials, as the athletes arrived for their events there was something amiss. The usual tense, testosterone-filled ambience of a major trial was absent with the atmosphere feeling relaxed, even jovial. Some of the sprinters strolled around in their sponsored tracksuits, merrily signing autographs and swanning around as if they knew something nobody else did.

> "It looked like a few athletes were given the nod about qualification for the Olympic relay without having to run at

> the trials even though we were told otherwise. It wasn't what we expected."
>
> — JASON GARDENER

For the bemused others, there was no time to seek clarification from any decision makers. There was a race to prepare for, one that would determine whether you went to the Olympics or not and finding the correct mental state to race was essential. Now that on the face of things some of the seats on the plane had already been filled, there would presumably be fewer places available through qualification at these trials. For some athletes, the tension and stress vanished whereas for others, the dial was turned up to ten.

All there was to do was to try and forget about the less-than-ideal circumstances and concentrate on the racing. Even if you were proven right, starting an argument with officials and selectors prior to any concrete outcomes wasn't the most prudent strategy if you wanted to be on the plane to Australia. The situation created an instant distrust in the process and a natural misgiving towards those people involved in it.

The Men's 100m final was one of the events affected by the developing politics but was still stacked with talent, with most of the aforementioned sprinters involved. It was won by Dwain Chambers with Darren Campbell in second and rather romantically, local Birmingham resident Mark Lewis-Francis in third. Alexander Stadium had gone from being a distant wonder for him, spied from the passenger seat of his dad's car, to being his stage to qualify for the biggest show in sport. Campbell strode to victory commandingly in the 200m event, with Marlon Devonish finishing third. Once the fun of the events had finished, the politically-charged fun of choosing the team started. The athletes were about to have their skepticism in the transparency of the process confirmed.

By finishing second in the 100m and first in the 200m, Darren Campbell was guaranteed selection for the Games in those events. His dominant performances in these trials had made things easy for the selectors while clearly he'd also be an asset for the relay team. This felt like an exciting time for Campbell.

He was about to get a lot more excitable in the stadium car park. Accosted by a UK Athletics official, he was told to his incredulity, that he would not be running both the 100m and the 200m at the Games while also competing in the relay.

This was no athlete-centred model of performance. Darren's goals were evidently not his to decide while his welfare was not his to discuss. He'd qualified under the existing rules for the right to contest three events and there had been no prior indication to any of the athletes of a greater strategy to compete at the relay. By rights, he'd be on the track for 3 events in Sydney but someone was pulling the rug out from under him. One of Britain's best hopes for a medal at the Games was being told to make do with two events rather than three.

The idea that this may have been a decision wrapped inside a greater vision was compromised by the fact that the conversation took place in the stadium car park, merely minutes after Campbell had qualified for the Olympic Games. Big decisions usually require strategic meetings rather than clandestine carpark rendezvous. The stench of hidden agendas and politics was exacerbated by the equally unfortunate aroma of poor planning and communication. This was looking messy.

The case for the defence for the officials lay in their presumption that Darren running three rounds for the relay as well as both individual events would place too heavy a burden on him. Usually three rounds, the big guns could be rested earlier on due to the stronger teams being diluted among different races, but with only two rounds, the stakes for qualification were higher. This was not Darren's problem. The officials should surely have been alive to the possibility that someone of Darren Campbell's calibre could potentially qualify for three events in Sydney and prepared for this eventuality.

Back in the car park, the goalposts for the officials moved once again. Campbell argued his case and protested the ridiculous nature of this situation to the official in question, the tone of his message straight from the streets of Moss Side. There was only one victor in this discussion. Darren Campbell would be running the 100m, 200m and the relay after all.

> "I told him that if the relay messed up and I was unable to run the 200m, it would all be on him, and I would see to it that people would know that."
>
> — Darren Campbell

To add melting icing to a rapidly burning cake, Mark Lewis-Francis had decided not to run at the Olympics despite qualifying for them. At merely seventeen years old, Mark's time would come.

The athletes arriving at these Olympic trials had been told that they would qualify for the relay team on merit but by this point, this concept was truly running on fumes. The opportunity to represent their nation in front of an audience of half a billion at the Olympic Games in the relay team was being doled out with haphazard planning and comedic politicking rather than being issued on sporting merit. The combination of egotistical, hyped up athletes with the opportunity of a lifetime on the line and a slovenly culture of officialdom, its procedures lacking in clarity or agility, made for a suspicious and antagonistic environment.

This atmosphere of distrust, selfishness and incompetence would lead to a logical conclusion.

THE OLYMPIC GAMES SYDNEY

Prior to each Olympic Games, there is a holding camp. Athletes arrive, acclimatise and prepare for the Games, usually in the same country but at least in the same time zone in order to allow the body a chance to freshen up and peak at the right time. Jason, Darren and Marlon were in Australia and were preparing for one of the high points of their lives.

Marlon Devonish was highly motivated for his first Olympic Games, to the extent that those around him were concerned that his training was a little too intense and that he was over-cooking things. Marlon had been desperate to get to Sydney and had been giving an extra 5-10% in training throughout the year to get him there. Keeping his foot on the accelerator caught up with him at the wrong time when he damaged his hamstring in a domestic race which only allowed him just over two weeks to get ready. His holding camp was focussed more on recovery than it was on performance which led some of the athletes behind him in the relay team pecking order to smell blood.

Due to the diligence of the medical staff and coaches, Marlon healed enough to get out on the track and perform. Whether he was healed enough to peak would be in the lap of the gods. As he walked out into the enormous Sydney Olympic Stadium towards the start of the Men's 200m heats, he was buzzing with excitement. On the night that Cathy Freeman won her gold in the 400m and Katharine Merry of the UK took the bronze, the stadium held a world record 112,524 spectators. The sheer volume of fans brought its own heat to an already baking and humid amphitheatre where unexpectedly, the Australian fans were cheering the British team whenever there wasn't a home athlete to support. The usual rivalries from cricket or rugby dissipated in the heat and there was a lot of love in the air from the Australian fans for the GB squad.

As Marlon sat in his blocks for the first heat, edgy and nervous for the first gun of his first Olympics, he felt his hamstring tweak. It was the worst possible feeling at the worst possible time. Even still, he had enough speed to qualify for the quarter finals. As he prepared his spikes and attached his numbers to his vest for the next round, he had the frustrating pleasure of watching Darren Campbell easily accelerate through to the semi-final, winning his quarter with a phenomenal time. Minutes later on the track, Marlon strained every sinew to emulate his British counterpart but, despite pushing his physical limits, he lacked strength and integrity in his hamstring. He was a Formula One car with a flat tyre. The relay didn't even cross his mind as he walked off the track into the tunnel, back to the medical room and onto the physio bed once more.

Dwain Chambers, Darren Campbell and Jason Gardener were Britain's representatives in the Men's individual 100m in Sydney. They all qualified easily from their morning heats in the searing sun but fate was not kind to Jason Gardener. He was drawn alongside World Championship silver and Olympic Gold medallist Bruny Surin, the soon-to-be World 100m champion Kim Collins and reigning World 200m champion and favourite for a Sydney 100m medal Ato Boldon. In the second round heats he was running against three people poised for podium finishes in the final. Jason had come close to breaking ten seconds a few weeks prior to the Olympics and needed this kind of performance merely to survive.

It was not to be. Jason finished fourth in his heat behind the trio, missing the fastest loser qualification spot by an agonising 0.03 seconds. Sport is ruthless and uncompromising when it comes to wider context and this result made Jason a mere statistic. He knew he was quick enough for the final but he started to realise that in major competitions, it wasn't all about the ability to run quickly just the once.

Dwain Chambers and Darren Campbell marched proudly on to the final as custodians of a new wave of British sprinting. Britain had been on the lookout for a new Linford Christie and it seemed three or four of them had arrived on the same plane. Britain had not had two men in the 100m final since Mike McFarlane and Donovan Reid at the Los Angeles 1984 Olympics, where Carl Lewis's exploits had inspired Darren and Jason Gardener to take up athletics in the first place. The American favourite Maurice Greene ultimately ran away with Ato Boldon for a sub-10 second gold and silver with Dwain and Darren fourth and sixth respectively, out of the medals but with their reputations as respected world class athletes solidified. Suddenly the formidable duo were heading up a firepower-laden crew of GB sprinters with the likes of Marlon Devonish, Jason Gardener, Ian Mackie, Allyn Condon and others also in Australia. The prospects looked mouthwatering for the British men's 4 x 100m relay team at Sydney.

The day before the first 4 x 100m heat, things got even better for fans of British sprinting as Darren Campbell won a sensational silver medal in the men's 200m behind the Greek athlete Konstantinos Kenteris. Campbell had powered around the bend and led the world with 40m to go, only for the white and blue vest of Greece to surge through and surprisingly win Olympic Gold. Nevertheless, Campbell had announced himself on to the world stage and in the process, had made a mockery of the supposed strategy to not allow him to double up on the sprint events.

If you had flown to Sydney as a member of the British relay team, it seemed now was a good time to be alive.

One of track and field's greatest assets as a spectacle is that everything is measured in time, distance or height, making things objective for both the competitor and spectator. There is no ambiguity and merit always prevails. In this respect, the selection calamity at Birmingham Alexander Stadium with some athletes informed of their selection before the trials, interfered with the essence of track and field. The mess and confusion at the birth of this Olympic relay team was to get worse on the other side of the world.

Anyone could see that this team was going to figure strongly in the final with a medal almost a certainty and consequently, everyone was desperate to make the final cut. The squad was larger than usual as a hedge against injury and while presumably the top places were cemented in the selectors' thoughts, team members lower in the depth chart became vocal, trying to complain and backbite their way into the team. The idea of meritocracy and any sense of perspective went out of the window and it became every man for himself now that there was a potential medal up for grabs.

> "It felt like a strong team on paper, but as soon as we were out there in Australia everyone suddenly became obsessed with their name being on the team sheet. The rivalry within

the team was almost more than the rivalries against the other countries."

— Marlon Devonish

The flickering flames of discontent within the relay team needed putting out. The problem was that while the fire had been started with the contentious approach of the officials at the Olympic trials, it was being fanned by the athletes at the Sydney Games. As if beating the other teams wasn't hard enough to begin with, the British team was busy defeating itself. British coach Steve Perks was a school headteacher by profession but even he found this competitive, motley crew of youths hard to handle. Some of the disruptive and rowdy boys at the back of the class were making it tough for the wider team to function.

The team was imploding. Bickering and bitterness became trademarks of what was supposed to be a cohesive team. Since Darren Campbell had run superbly to win a silver medal in the Men's 200m, he and fellow finalist Christian Malcolm were rested for the relay heats. This led to another bout of in-fighting because whoever would be chosen in Darren's place for the heat would presumably be dropped for the final. That person became Jason Gardener who had qualified for the Olympics by right in the individual 100m. Jason felt there was political favouritism at play and things almost came to blows between the British athletes and staff in front of the other teams on the warm up track.

On paper the GB relay team in Sydney was very strong but individuals were creaking physically and psychologically. Team spirit had evaporated and there was no psychological safety, no understanding and no mutual belief. The athletes could hardly look each other in the eye. The team became a mess of mistrust, misunderstanding and ultimately, missed baton exchanges.

Allyn Condon, Jason Gardener, Marlon Devonish and Dwain Chambers were selected as the team for the heats but this was no team. This was just four athletes selected, leaving others bitter and spiteful that they hadn't been. A lack of team cohesion, unclear definition of roles and woeful communication led to the athletes looking shockingly amateur in front of a worldwide audience, exiting the relay competition in the first round. One could easily imagine the non-selected athletes on the sidelines laughing in their sleeves, quietly celebrating the failure of their own team.

Hindsight would allow all involved to see the situation for what it was – slower members of the team causing chaos so that they might leave the Olympics with a medal they wouldn't have dreamed of obtaining weeks previously. Many of the athletes had been part of successful relay squads and the fringe element hedged their bets on it happening in Sydney.

Back in Birmingham, England, Mark Lewis-Francis watched all this unfold on his family's television. He saw the team self-destruct, knowing he would have been at those very Olympics had he and his coach Steve Platt decided not to concentrate on a greater vision, with Mark's future interests and welfare at heart. In reality, he wasn't ready for that kind of pressure and scrutiny from commentators or fans; that would come in time, whether he merited it or not. Fellow athletes, other coaches and friends kept telling him that he should have gone to the Games, but he trusted his coach and he trusted the plan, even if many around him failed to realise the value of this approach at the time.

As he watched the calamity in Sydney unfurl from the comfort of his sofa, Mark felt truly awful for his fellow athletes. He felt that he was on the cusp of becoming a part of something bigger and was invested in the success of his peers. His own career was blossoming, but the larger picture for him was being accepted into a cohort of people who he had respected and looked up to for years.

> "When I watched all that happen on TV, my immediate thoughts went to those that had advised me that I could wait until another Olympics were right. Athletically I was ready for an Olympic Games, but I realised there and then that I wasn't quite ready to have to deal with everything that went with it off the track [laughs]."
>
> Mark Lewis-Francis

What he saw from afar was the dreams of people he admired being extinguished and them being castigated for it. The political intricacies of the behind-the-scenes-mess didn't transmit through his television but he saw the end result of it in the same way that everyone else did. If he hadn't appreciated the sheer heat that could be generated in the crucible of high performance, he did now.

The press had a field day and who could blame them? As a heavily-funded Lottery money initiative (as athletics was at this time), this public humiliation made the stakeholders doubt the entire enterprise. The concept of the relay team and everything associated with it became toxic. In a sport where individual successes existed alongside those of team successes, personal rivalries became a warm comfort blanket to which one could return to focus on their own career and stay well clear of the mess of getting four people together to win together. Competing with and beating one another became a place of safety. Why entertain the notion of winning together? Down that path lay argument, dysfunction and failure.

TWENTY DAYS LATER MARK LEWIS FRANCIS RAN 10.12 SECONDS in being crowned World Junior Champion at the Estadio Nacional, Santiago, Chile. He and his coach had evidently made a very smart choice.

5

JASON GARDENER

> "Being mixed race ensured that I was standing out from the crowd but at the same time not really knowing where I was fitting in."
>
> — Jason Gardener

During the late 1970s and early 80s, the county of Somerset welcomed the cricketing greats Viv Richards and Joel Garner to their ranks. Richards was a magnetic personality and a showman who used the cricket bat as a medium to achieve a greatness that transcended sport. Being from the city of Bath and a keen sports fan, Jason Gardener became enamoured with brilliant sportspeople such as Richards, athlete Daley Thompson and footballer John Barnes. They were sportsmen at the very top of their game who were the same colour as him.

As a nine-year-old, he sat glued to his television as the 1984 Los Angeles Olympics were beamed in kaleidoscopic glory from the mock-Roman Los Angeles Coliseum. From the opening ceremony's jet-packed rocket-man to the world's flags displayed throughout the stadium by the crowd, the spectacle made it impossible for an impressionable kid not to be wowed. As Britain's Daley Thompson and American sprinter Carl Lewis stole the show, Jason was hooked.

A couple of hundred miles to the north, a young Darren Campbell was watching those same Games, transfixed by the heroic exploits of Lewis and Ed Moses. Campbell's hero was Jesse Owens and Lewis, by emulating Owen's feat of four golds at the same Games, instantly became a touchstone figure for both Gardener and Campbell. They switched off their televisions at the end of those Olympics and decided that they were going to go to the Olympic Games. Their journey to win Olympic gold together started there and then.

WITH A WHITE MOTHER AND A BLACK FATHER, JASON AND SISTER Jessica didn't look like other people in Bath. This was an era and a geographical location where mixed relationships were unusual making it a confusing time for the siblings at school and elsewhere. The white side of the family was nurturing, protective and loving; the black side of the family was equally as loving but tougher and harsher in its delivery of that love. The idea was to prepare the children to do tough jobs and accept the racially-biased glass ceiling that would inevitably come their way. It was a way of preparing the children for their journeys.

One of Jason Gardener's teachers at school was at worst a racist, at best a bigot. Her treatment was extended to any child different to the mostly white, middle class kids at the school. One Italian boy in Jason's class suffered similar mistreatment to Jason with, 'Go back to your own country' being the standard innuendo. When these behaviours came from those in positions of authority at the school, it gave a green light to others to follow suit. School was a tough time for Jason Gardener.

Low in confidence and lacking encouragement at school, Jason had the potential to be disruptive and disinterested in equal measure. He'd grown accustomed to never quite fitting in, wherever he was and in time, this sense of displacement led to a lack of self-confidence and a surplus of anxiety. He was never bottom of the class academically but he was never far from it. The only thing that gave him a lift was that he seemed a little quicker than the others when it came to ball sports. This wasn't much but given that he found encouragement hard to come by elsewhere, it was an important trickle of self-esteem in an otherwise barren environment.

He was so very nervous at his first school sports day. Here was an event, the school's own Olympic finals day, where classroom champions would be crowned. If you won, you could claim the title of 'fastest in the class' for an entire calendar year. This was Jason's first experience with placing consequence on his talents. The school grass track had might as well been a packed coliseum, with the sounds and aromas of competition filling his senses. He wore a pristine white kit and spent the morning equally anxious and excited. Here was an opportunity to be able to demonstrate his one ability to his peers. His classmates suddenly became rivals in other lanes, as if from other nations. Here his detachment became an advantage, his opponents not there to be acknowledged or spoken to, merely threats to be extinguished.

As he settled on the start line, Jason felt the sensation of complete, hushed silence for the first time. The only sound he could hear was his heart in his throat. The whistle went and he immediately ran away from his classmates within the first few metres. The rest of the race lasted a lifetime. He spent every stride until crossing the finish line petrified that he would either fall over on the undulating grass surface or get caught.

Winning the race etched in his memory the feeling of being good at something but even more than that, having his ability recognised by others. Being congratulated and celebrated by his peers and teachers was a new experience for Jason.

He wanted to hold on to that feeling.

That warm summer's day, Jason's peers sat up and took notice. He'd become the fast kid. While he enjoyed being celebrated for a change, developing a reputation for being good at running swung a double-edged sword, boosting his self-esteem while also attaching this new confidence to his athletic ability. This green shoot of aptitude did little to ease Jason's anxiety or halt the perpetual and normalised racism he experienced at school.

One day a nun, Sister Mary O'Dowd, took notice of Jason's talents outside of the class and contrasted them to his wasted talents inside of the class. Sister Mary brought some medals into school and remarked to young Jason that if he became a good student and worked hard, perhaps he could win a few himself, through sport or otherwise. At the time he was dealing with his own contrasts; in skin colour, in abilities in school and now in how people treated him. On one hand there was the casually cruel racism of his bigoted teacher and on the other, kindness and encouragement from Sister Mary. It made him realise how much being praised made a difference in how he felt and how he behaved. It also brought into sharp focus how the daily cruelty and ignorance he'd experienced had shaped his attitudes up to that point. Sister Mary's attitude was a beacon of light and she taught him more about the association between hard work and success through a word of encouragement and showing him those medals than he'd learned in any of his lessons up to that point.

A couple of hundred miles up the road in Ashton-on-Mersey in Manchester, young Darren Campbell was also struggling through his own experience of misbehaviour and unruly behaviour at school. He was equally as uninterested as Jason in the constant racism associated with being a minority black presence at school and fought back with his own aggression and academic apathy. He also encountered a positive role model to modify his views. Dave Law, a strong-minded alpha male presence in the school faculty, slowly brought to Darren's attention the opportunities he had through his athletic abilities and how he could be the master of his own fate. He brought an equal measure of praise and consequence where others had only brought punishment and encouragement where others had brought ear-bashing. Jason and Darren didn't yet know each other, but they already had a shared history in the making.

Jason joined the City of Bath Amateur Athletic Club and immediately found success. He was already quicker than many of the established athletes at the club and when he was selected to represent the County of Avon at the English Schools Championships at Hull in 1992, he was confident of excelling. When he finished third in his first heat and seventh in the semi-final he was absolutely crestfallen. This was supposed to be the thing he was really good at. He wasn't academically inclined and wanted more than anything to emulate his sporting heroes, posters of whom now adorned his bedroom walls. The sheer speed and calibre of the other athletes took him by surprise. He had no idea people could be so much quicker than him and it hurt. He realised he had a choice. He could wallow in his anguish at not being up to the standard and quit or he could roll up his sleeves and work harder than ever before. There was no way he'd continue to run if it was going to be like this. He either had to work hard and get better, or quit.

Momentarily, future Olympic medallist Jason Gardener considered giving up athletics. The experience in Hull was a painful one but it wouldn't be his last. He was also playing football at a good level, enjoying success with his breakneck speed. He was invited for trials with Bristol Rovers and this provided an injection of self-confidence and further confirmation of his sporting talents. This didn't last long with Gardener joining a long and illustrious list of promising footballers not deemed good enough to make the final cut. The knockbacks came thick and fast. The parallel path with Campbell, who left athletics to play football for Plymouth for a period, continued and they could feasibly had played against one another in a West Country Bristol Rovers v Plymouth Argyle derby in 2004 instead of pursuing their Olympic dreams in Athens. His football escapades showed Jason how little control an individual had in a team sport, where coaches' selections often determined and shaped careers. He wanted control of his own destiny and for that process to be objective and unequivocally fair. Track and field, measured against a stopwatch or tape measure, gave him this power. He decided to commit to athletics.

The experience in Hull at the English Schools had taught Jason one very important lesson. There were other athletes out there and to improve, he had to widen his gaze. He took on the advice of Peter Roscoe, a friend's father who became another father figure. They sought out better competitions of a higher standard where Jason would have to run quickly merely to compete. The South West was a sleepy and underdeveloped area for athletics at the time, so every weekend they packed up Mr Roscoe's car, clocking up thousands of miles traveling the country to compete in junior competitions. One such event was held in Telford, just to the north-west of

Birmingham where as a fourteen-year-old, Jason Gardener ran against one of the quicker runners in the Midlands at the time. He was an athlete from Coventry and his name was Marlon Devonish.

> "More than anything else in the world, I wanted to be coached by a serious and successful coach - someone who would take me seriously and help me succeed."
>
> — Jason Gardener

Jason's Auntie Sue used to tell her brother Dave that 'our Jason is a good runner'. Being a specialist pole vault coach associated with British Athletics, Dave Lease was well-accustomed to humouring testimonies about someone's family member or friend in the local area with talent. Nevertheless, Dave looked into Jason's performances and kept an interest in the times that Gardener was posting in age group races. There came a point that these performances brought his opinion in line with his sister's. Jason was showing evidence of being actually half decent.

At sixteen, Jason performed poorly in his GCSE exams, attaining grades reflective of his interest and application. He was lined up to be a car mechanic. This is where the intervention from coach Lease proved life changing. Dave Lease immediately unlocked the potential in his young athlete not by merely improving his athletic ability, but by showing Jason that he could apply himself with focus and diligence when the end goal justified those means. Lease told Jason that he needed to retake his GCSEs if he wanted to pursue athletics.

Dave Lease's entire career in and out of sport was grounded in the formula of applied work and structure, as well as planning for success. He saw a disconnect between Jason's obvious ability to focus and apply himself in sport with his inability to do this when it came to academia. Lease was also experienced enough to know that it was the latter that provided a more stable platform in life, given that a career in athletics was both unlikely and underpaid. Lease made a bargain with Jason; if Jason improved his grades, Lease would take him on as an athlete.

Jason could not believe his ears. He wanted to work with an experienced, Olympic-level coach like Dave Lease more than anything in the world. He made the deal enthusiastically. This was the start of something for Gardener who began to believe he could achieve anything if his desire was strong enough. The aspiration to be coached by Lease was overwhelming and he honoured his part of the bargain through determination, work ethic, and the belief and confidence Lease had given him[1].

Lease immediately started to educate his young protégé on the intricacies of technical perfection, strength development and about the importance of power-to-weight ratio and conditioning. He gave him a plan to follow on his own with the promise of revisiting things together on an ad hoc basis to fit in with each other's schedules. Gardener followed this plan religiously. Within the space of about four months, Jason won a silver in the English Indoor Championships, beating some very quick people along the way. He could not believe his own improvement. Significantly, neither could Lease. He had seen so many things during his coaching career that he had forgotten more than many coaches ever learned but he knew that to see this kind of improvement so quickly was rare. Dave Lease was experienced enough and intelligent enough to know that this was worthy of his attention.

The combination of passion, focus and determination was a prerequisite for any athlete but Gardener was extremely meticulous. He approached his training as if he simply could not afford to fail. There was an element of overcompensation in this attitude to combat a constant feeling that with historical selections to most teams going to the kids from big cities, Jason needed to work harder than everyone else. Having had his self-esteem knocked when he was confident at the English Schools and having already faced rejection through the experience at Bristol Rovers, Gardener's underdog attitude could be turned into a strength. He was hungry to prove a point. Lease combined Jason's drive with his own forensic coaching detail and the two of them aligned perfectly.

The delight of achieving his first international junior GB vest was tempered with the disappointment of failing to make the European Junior Championship, but a theme was emerging which was to repeat itself through his career; he found that a temporary low was always a catalyst to propel himself to new heights. He was chosen for the 1994 World Junior Championships in Portugal where he won a silver in the 100m and a gold in the 4 x 100m. This was the start of his GB relay journey for in that same relay squad was Marlon Devonish and Ian Mackie, all guided by future senior Olympic team relay coach Steve Perks. Jason and Marlon started to know each other's idiosyncrasies very early indeed.

> "Almost immediately I realised that I was much a threat to their place on the team as much as I was a team-mate."
>
> — Jason Gardener

Jason's posters on his wall included John Regis, Linford Christie and Colin Jackson, all saved cut outs or centre page spreads from newspapers or Athletics Weekly magazine. They were his inspiration. When he got drafted to his first senior international at the 1995 European Cup event at Villeneuve D'Ascq, near Lille in France, he was star-struck as much as he was struck by nerves. Here was the relay team of his childhood idols and him. Christie, Braithwaite, Jarrett, Jackson and Gardener. He went to the event as a spare relay runner but due to an injury to Colin Jackson, he was promoted into the team itself. He was in heaven but at the same time, he felt far removed from being a part of the team, as much of an outsider as he had felt growing up in Bath. The cliques and mini-fraternities which existed in track and field were hard to break into and there was no arm around the new young member. Each new athlete was a threat, a potential competitor, a rival in all but name.

The dream of lining up alongside his childhood heroes was turning into an anxious experience for the youngster keen to impress. The reason for this anxiety was simple. Gardener was diligent, keen on practice and detail and in this cohort he was the new guy. He wanted to ensure that he played his part and played it well. He wanted to integrate and do his job. Being fresh to the environment, he was unprepared for the role he was being asked to fulfil. This was his first senior GB vest and he felt that the timings and speeds of the relay baton changeovers needed to be rehearsed before being exposed in front of an audience of tens of thousands and millions of viewers on television.

Yet the others didn't really do relay practice. There was a jog, a handover and a brief description of the process and logistics a couple of hours before the start of the race. It was preparation in name only. The level of detail assigned to the skill of high-speed baton changing was rudimentary to say the least, the relay rehearsal nothing more than a box-ticking exercise. Gardener started to worry. If he was a part of a British relay team which failed to get the baton around, his heroes were going to crucify him on day one.

Any athlete new to the group was an outsider until they proved otherwise. There was no red carpet welcome or gentle introduction to alleviate anxiety or to get the best from the newcomer. People might not even shake your hand. The body language from the incumbents said, "This is our team. Just because someone else has chosen you doesn't mean we accept you." New members often felt deeply unwelcome.

Luckily – and it truly was as much luck as it was judgment considering the amount of practice involved - the baton was handed on from Gardener to Tony Jarrett before continuing around the track to win the race. The sense of relief overcame any joy for Jason. He had won his first senior international race but the experience left him perplexed and concerned. The team's procedures had made him feel vulnerable at a time that he should have been thinking of nothing but his own performance and he felt that he'd succeeded despite the environment rather than because of it. He left Lille thinking if he ever became a senior figure in the relay team, that team would be nothing but exceptionally well-prepared.

> "We had this rather strange custom in training, almost from day one, where we would practice relay handovers. It was done with the attitude behind it of 'You'll never know when you'll need it."
>
> — Jason Gardener

Jason and Dave Lease practiced the relay "push-pass" handover almost every day, both receiving and exchanging the baton. This left many an onlooker bemused but meticulous planner Lease had the foresight to predict that a diminutive powerful starter would someday, somewhere, need to be familiar with the skill of relay baton changes. Intuition and outside-the-box thinking led to one of Britain's most promising athletes becoming very comfortable with the basic schoolboy skill of baton running as a part of his training. Such a thing was considered too ordinary for advanced athletes but Lease saw fit to prepare his charge for any future possibilities. Gardener struggled to reconcile his own attentiveness to what seemed like a key skill with its apparent absence at the highest level.

At this time, a school teacher from West Wales by the name of Steve Perks took on the responsibility of the senior British relay coach's role having achieved success at junior level where one of his charges had been Jason Gardener. One of the more striking aspects of the relay culture that met Perks head-on was this laissez-faire attitude towards changeover practice and technical mastery of the event. Not only did he believe that the attitude needed to change in order to achieve success, he saw that the entire relay event was regarded by the athletes themselves as something between 'fun' and 'added-extra.' Perks and Gardener were entering the same den at the same time and what they saw surprised both of them.

Two months after returning from Lille, the 1995 World Athletics Championships were held in Gothenburg, Sweden and Gardener was once again taken as a relay squad member. History repeated itself, with an injury to Linford Christie promoting Jason into the relay team. The team failed to function as a cohesive unit and was disqualified in the semi-final, leading many of the senior members to blame Gardener's inexperience. Nineteen-year-old Jason took this unwarranted criticism personally, returning home and ripping down the posters that adorned his bedroom wall. The idols had become rivals.

TWO DECADES LATER, THE VICE-CHANCELLOR'S CHRISTMAS drinks at the University of Bath brought together the academic faculty as well as individuals from the wider community. Local academics and local Olympic Champions were mingling. Jason Gardener, by now an MBE and having been given the Freedom of his home City the City of Bath, got talking to the chaplain of the University, Father Bill. They discussed many things, from Jason's upbringing at a Catholic school to the chaplain's interest in sport. A few weeks passed, until Jason received an email from the chaplain referencing an article from 1999 where he had spoken about Sister Mary O'Dowd and her positive influence on him as a young man. Sister Mary was still alive and Father Bill's intervention put them back in touch in what was an emotionally-charged experience for Gardener. Yet it was not to end there. Prior to the London 2012 Olympic Games, again through the chaplain's intervention, Jason found himself in St.Peter's Basilica, Vatican City, in a private audience with the pope.

The boy that endured racism at a Catholic school was now a Member of the British Empire meeting the Holy See.

6

"The strength of the team is each individual member. The strength of each member is the team."

— PHIL JACKSON

Phil Jackson, the coach of the dominant Chicago Bulls basketball team of the late nineties, not only had a way with words, but was a true pioneer of his profession. He was fortunate to have the guile of Scottie Pippen, the hustle of Dennis Rodman and the genius of Michael Jordan executing his game plan meaning that this Bulls team had a combination of exceptional talent and strong guidance. Jordan's once-in-a-generation fusion of athletic ability and preternatural understanding of the sport were maximised by the complementary skill sets of the other Bulls players.

The same principle applied with the Manchester United football team under Sir Alex Ferguson. Characters as different as Andrew Cole, Eric Cantona and Roy Keane all thrived in a team crafted over years, with homegrown players like Ryan Giggs, David Beckham and Paul Scholes periodically augmented by the likes of Ruud van Nistelrooy and Dwight Yorke.

Phil Jackson pieced together a jigsaw, with excellent individuals fulfilling specific roles within the coach's structured framework; Dennis Rodman was the out-and-out rebounder, Scottie Pippen the league's best wingman on offense and defense, while everyone orbited and complemented the greatest player in the game in Michael Jordan. Alex Ferguson on the other hand painted an evolving picture where Keane, Scholes, Beckham and Giggs were equally adept at covering for one another as well as playing within the framework created for them. Giggs especially, could be a skilful and speedy winger in one game and a central midfielder reliant on vision and execution the next. Keane was a ferociously competitive midfielder yet could slice the opposition's defence in half with delicate feather-touch passing or even chip in with the odd crucial goal, most famously against Juventus in Turin.

Looking at these two teams with the benefit of hindsight and remarking on their qualities isn't hard. In fact, appraising winning teams and reverse-engineering their supposed virtues is easy. Creating that winning team is far more difficult. Whether it's a jigsaw or an oil painting, 'What creates a winning team?' is obsessed over by football managers to world leaders, from Barack Obama to Brian Clough. The answer to this question is the holy grail of sport, business or even society as a whole. The answer needs to have a clear mission, strong leadership, account for the different people involved and for the most part, be lucky. You might be able to recognise a great team once it exists but bringing that team into existence is a far tougher task. Being a food critic doesn't make you a chef.

A track and field sprint relay team is not a team like any other. To even call it a team is something of a paradox, for a relay quartet is made up of a collection of four competing rivals who compete against one another for individual glory for most of their careers. For the majority of the time, members of this 'team' are existential threats to each other's income streams, successes and personal ambitions.

> "Darren and I were always rivals as much as peers, and competitive enemies as much as we were friends."
>
> — Jason Gardener

Marlon Devonish was a constant threat to Darren Campbell's dreams. Darren in turn was an ever-present handbrake on all of Jason Gardener's aspirations. Mark Lewis-Francis's arrival on the scene as a young upstart threatened to usurp and prematurely end the careers of all three. To add another problem to the mix for this already threadbare notion of a team, mere weeks before being moulded into an elite unit tasked to compete on the highest stage, all potential members would be intense rivals actively looking to deprive the others of qualification for that very team. Conceiving a unified and driven unit emerging from this troubled genesis was an exercise in hope over design. Anything built on such a foundation of competing agendas would be a castle built on very fine sand indeed.

Most teams in professional working environments are crafted with foresight and strategy. Take the process of advertising for a job. The application stage of the journey screens for proficiency and suitability for a role while the interview applies some pressure and gives the team-builder the opportunity to assess the soft skills and fit of the candidate. This even happens to a lesser extent within the recruitment phase of team sports, where the game of bluff and leverage played by agents is countered with enquiry, analysis and background research by the teams looking to add the right talent to their mix. Character and fit are extremely important in these processes.

By contrast, relay teams were rivals that were expected to cease hostilities immediately and get along. There was no considering the suitability of personality traits to work with one another as qualification was based on speed in the trials, the obvious meritocracy of the sport perhaps even hindering potential team building. Then there was no chance for long-term planning or succession strategy for the simple reason that the time between qualifying for the team and standing on the start line to compete was just over a month.

> "Members of a relay team are different in what they can offer. In the same way that defenders in football have slightly different habits, mindsets and traits to attackers, different legs of a sprint relay have different demands."
>
> — Darren Campbell

The four individual legs of a relay team constitute four different skill sets and even suit different mindsets. The first leg requires a recognised starter – something not as prevalent in sprinting as one would imagine. This leg requires a powerful athlete, possessing rapid acceleration (which is different to the ability to run at full speed), while also having a capacity to gain speed while running in a curve around a bend. This is why many recognised 60m indoor sprinters naturally gravitate to this role. For the British team the 110m hurdler Colin Jackson, recognised as one of the fastest starters in the world during his illustrious career, filled this role on many occasions. To complement these physical requirements, the first leg athlete also needs a strong and calm mindset to be able to cope with nerves and the temperament to handle the potential false starts that a race with 32 athletes could have. Lastly, the baton handover from bend to straight is a skill which is exceptionally easy to get wrong. It is not too dissimilar to a docking sequence in space where two rapidly moving objects travel in the same direction but not necessarily on the same trajectory and need to merge at a point. For those that baulk and scold athletes at their supposed inability to 'get the baton around', if that were the objective of the exercise it could be easily done in around fifty seconds or so. Getting it around in thirty-eight seconds is a high-risk game of probabilities on the outer limits of human performance. The margins for error are so small that all actions from running to timings exist light years away from any comfort zone.

The second leg is more suited to an athlete with a high top-end speed. During this leg, the baton travels well over 100m in the hands of the athlete from reception to delivery, suiting those with elevated levels of speed endurance. Without this fortitude, the handover to the third runner sees a tiring athlete with dissipating energy levels attempting to catch up with an explosive take-off from the next runner - a recipe for an out-of-box change or dropped baton if there ever was one. Historically for the British team, the second leg had favoured athletes such as Darren Campbell, Christian Malcolm and John Regis. Their abilities to excel at the 200m as well as the 100m gave them sufficient fuel to sustain their speed over the long back straight and maintain it as the race drew past halfway to the final bend. This end of the second leg is where many teams fall out of contention as the stagger starts to unwind and as the bottleneck of the third leg builds up the pressure. A poor performance towards the end of the second leg could nullify one team, while a strong performance could turbocharge another. Possessing calmness at very high speed and an ability to execute handling and receiving the baton while in full flight is a prerequisite here.

While the first leg involves accelerating into a bend, the third leg involves the complex skill of leaning into a curve while already travelling at high speed. This places maximum physical demands on the core, the athlete's centre of gravity, and on ankle strength. A single step out of line can easily lead to fishtailing like an aquaplaning car, momentum inexorably pulling the athlete out of their lane. This leg is akin to sprinting across a curved tightrope. Coolness under pressure is paramount, for the athlete can see the race unravel before their eyes, needing to resist a compulsion to panic or the temptation to seize an opportunity as they realise their position in the field. Like the golfer on top of the leaderboard teeing off on the final hole or the striker lining up a match-winning penalty in the final minute, the consequences of their performance on the team's result is painfully apparent to the third leg runner. The sights and sounds of the athletes around them can indicate their position in the race at this point and they become acutely aware of the team's standing as they close in on the final athlete ahead of them.

The last leg of the sprint relay needs a finisher; an Alan Shearer, Michael Jordan or Bryan Habana. Someone with an eye and an instinct for getting over the line above all else. The last leg is one for the sprinting purist – a rush for glory powered by aggression and sheer competitive will. Psychologically, all the legs require an athlete not fazed by pressure but the mental effort for the anchor runner is carried in the minutes leading up to the event itself. Traditionally, this leg is where the sprinting heavyweights of the world converge. This runner stands with superstars, big names and medal winners. For the uninitiated, it is all too easy to be intimidated by some of the most well-known athletes in the world stood right next to you, pacing menacingly in their lanes before settling to await the baton. The big guns make it their business to get into their opponents' heads in order to empty them of confidence. The mental warfare and posturing that occurs on the top of the home straight during the relay is the same as before a heavyweight boxing match. Not only do the athletes actively seek to make one another nervous, the sheer gravity of what is at stake between their position on the bend and the finish line creates a high wire tension. The temptation for athletes to get away early is enormous and staying focussed with medals on the line is physically and mentally draining.

Far from being four athletes merely running as quickly as possible and handing each other a metal stick, the constituent parts of a relay team involves many moving parts as well as one rapidly moving baton. It needs humans to run as smoothly as a Swiss watch and as fast as a race car. If you were to apply this description to one man, no one in the history of athletics could suit it better than Usain Bolt.

BERLIN 2009
WORLD CHAMPIONSHIPS

The Olympiastadion in Berlin was built by Adolf Hitler's national socialist party as the stage for the Third Reich propaganda festival that was the 1936 Berlin Olympics. Jesse Owens, of course, wonderfully disassembled that constructed myth. The stadium in the western suburbs of Berlin still stands as a monument to sport and to history.

Marlon Devonish had finished his individual warm-up and was in the call-up room. He took off his headphones, packed them away in his kitbag and prepared to walk around the back straight of this daunting arena to his start position in the 2009 World Championships relay final.

He gazed around at his surroundings, marvelling at the newly constructed roof which shielded athletes and fans from the rain and shouldered the historical weight of past events. A new chapter of the stadium's legacy had been written days previously, when Usain Bolt from Jamaica had run a scarcely believable 9.58 seconds for the 100m, demolishing his own world record in the process and making the superstars of yesteryear seem vaguely pedestrian in comparison. Both Marlon and Usain were about to run the third leg of the men's 4 x 100m relay semi-final. This was surprising. Usain Bolt wasn't just the fastest man in the world at the time, he was the fastest human being that had ever lived. He would surely be on the last leg, or failing that, the second, 'long' leg of the relay? He'd run the last leg a year prior at the Beijing Olympic Games and that had ended very well for him and the Jamaican team.

Marlon chatted to Usain as they walked from the warm up to their start point. He asked him, why was he running the third leg? The answer was simple. Usain didn't like running with the baton in his left hand. The Jamaicans put him on the third leg so that the baton would be in his right hand.

There was no ego from Bolt. No grandstanding or glory-hunting. He simply adapted to what was best for the group. Within the Jamaican team, it made sense to make the quickest man ever feel comfortable for him to run his best race, wherever that was. This also ensured the same privilege for the other athletes. They wouldn't have to compromise their own preferences or change their habits to engineer having Bolt run on the last leg. He was happy to take the third leg and leave the glory of the finish to someone better suited to it. Simple team strategy won over all else.

7

3 YEARS TO GO
EDMONTON WORLD ATHLETICS CHAMPIONSHIPS
2001

"It honestly felt like nothing was going on there."

— Mark Lewis-Francis

The 2001 World Athletics Championships were held in Edmonton, Canada. The athletes called the place 'Dead-monton'. There was an airport to fly into, there was a hotel to stay in and there was a stadium to compete in. That was pretty much it. There was none of the celebratory feel usually present at high level competitions, no joyous festival atmosphere. The fact that the host country failed to win a single medal in any of the men's or women's events contributed to a feeling of apathy from the home crowd. The epicentre of the ice hockey world tried to embrace track and field for a few weeks but without home nation expertise, the passion necessary for a memorable competition never materialised.

This lack of enthusiasm was amplified when even reliable Canadian athletes like Donovan Bailey failed to make an impression with Diane Cummings's 5th position in the women's 800m being Canada's best performance in their home games. An underwhelming spectacle became something soon to forget for the host nation. The party had started but the front door was left open, with the hosts checking their watches instead of refilling champagne glasses.

Despite the lacklustre atmosphere, on the morning of 11th August 2001 at these Edmonton World Championships, the British team were giddy with excitement at the prospect of what was to come from their men's 4 x 100m relay quartet. Both Christian Malcolm and Dwain Chambers had reached the final of the 100m and Malcolm and Marlon Devonish both qualified for the 200m final. To add to this potent mix, Mark Lewis-Francis had posted a sub-10 second 100m days earlier in a windy quarter final even if the wind proved to be frustrating +0.1 metres/second above the legal limit. Nevertheless, the British sprinters were firing. None had won a medal but in terms of consistency and the ability to replicate results, this kind of strength in depth was normally the preserve of the American or Jamaican teams.

By this time, Marlon Devonish had won his own individual medals and was beginning to get a name as a pedigree relay runner, even if he wasn't yet in a position where he could be involved in big decisions or influence the relay group. He had ground his way through the heats to reach the World Championship final in the 200m but had simply ran out of steam in the chase for medals. Nevertheless his performances were testament to the fact that he belonged at the top table of world sprinting. Even though this World Championships had a distinct paint-by-numbers feel to it, the performances of the British sprinters suggested that a relay medal was a very real possibility.

For Mark Lewis-Francis, these were his very first senior championships. Having run so quickly in his heats against a field that included Bruni Surin and Obadele Thompson, these championships had the potential to be a breakout for him. There was no pressure on him to deliver but in running so quickly so early, he inadvertently invited the spotlight to be placed on him. Donovan Bailey, one of Lewis-Francis's heroes growing up, was paying him compliments in the media which delighted Mark almost as much as running 'sub-ten'. Dwain Chambers and Christian Malcolm qualified for the final, ensuring half of a potential British relay team competing for podium positions in the individual 100m event.

Mark's journey to the final had momentum but he agonisingly missed out on qualifying by one place having finished fifth in his semi-final. This was a personal disappointment but a good lesson on the intricacies and physical demands of multi-round events at major championships. One important lesson that hit home was that if he truly was serious about medaling, he needed to manage his physical energy levels and emotional arousal in the earlier rounds. If he could get to the semi-final able to operate at 95-98%, he could be safe in the knowledge that his performance in the final would be even quicker. Mark had emptied the tank too early and coming to this understanding would pay dividends later in his career. He was accruing a growing bank of experience for one still very young.

Another new experience was being left out of the relay team, despite having run fast enough to justify selection. Was he dropped? Was he rested? Or had he been omitted for greater strategic reasons? He wasn't quite sure. What he was sure of was that he was watching from the sidelines.

There was a back story behind Mark Lewis Francis's non-selection which had almost nothing to do with athletic performance or even the ability to run quickly. It begins with the decision to appoint Steve Perks as coach of the senior UK relay team back in 1997. Here was a teacher with a Richard Burton-esque Welsh accent who was under scrutiny almost from the moment he was appointed. Despite enjoying successes at world level with the junior setup, many coaches and ex-athletes that had coveted his job felt aggrieved that a perceived outsider in the UK athletics fraternity had been bestowed with such a prestigious role. Furthermore, Perks could never entertain the notion of a full-time job in athletics since it was too fragile, precarious and frankly didn't pay anywhere near as much as his career in education. In time, he would find himself the only non-professional coach in the GB coaching setup, requiring the blessing of his own school's board of governors in order to attend world sporting spectacles that those governors would enjoy at home on their televisions. The role became a labour of love with late nights, missed family weekends and very little free time left over. There were very few perks to Steve's job.

Family commitments led to him not being a part of the coaching staff that had travelled to Edmonton. From a strategic point of view, this was quite a hurdle to overcome. It may feel foreign now in our interconnected world where we can speak to people on the other side of the world in ultra-high definition, but this was before FaceTime, Zoom and WhatsApp, when even email was in its infancy. Intercontinental conversations were held over fuzzy phone lines at two dollars per minute. Whether the coaches and officials liked it or not, this is how selection and strategic decisions were communicated in Edmonton.

With Steve Perks four thousand miles away, the coaches and officials on the ground were developing their own opinions and susceptible to being influenced by those around them. There were coaches, athletes, ex-athletes and agents (sometimes all rolled up in the form of one person) on site who were keen to get their opinions heard. Rumours of an athlete being fresher, more experienced or in better form than another served to cloud instead of clarify selection. In the midst of all the competing narratives swirling around team selection ultimately, John Barbour found himself anchoring the relay.

Whatever the reasons for selection, there were still four or five individuals at the top of their game. If they could gel as a cohesive unit, the medal rostrum was waiting for them. Jason Gardener and Darren Campbell had sat out almost the entire 2001 season with injuries so the team could not rely on continuity of selection. On the flip side, the quality of the individual performers was high and while the press and supporters busied themselves hypothetically jigsawing together potential British teams, the team itself was preparing to make the Sydney calamity of the previous year a distant memory.

In the last relay heat of the day, the British team were readying themselves for what would surely be a formality against the likes of Israel, Mauritius, South Africa and the Ivory Coast. The team that was chosen was a strong one for a heat. The favoured nations for medals tended to be confident in their ability to reach a final operating below maximum capacity and would rest their quicker runners, trusting in the squad's strength in depth. Britain however were taking no chances in the quest for this relay final. With recent failures in mind, there was a determination to avoid a repeat of Sydney. All three finalists from the individual sprint events were chosen for the first three legs with young up-and-comer John Barbour on the anchor leg, chosen ahead of Mark Lewis-Francis despite the latter's blistering 9.97 seconds performance in the individual heats for the 100m.

Dwain Chambers and Marlon Devonish got the team off to a strong start and when handing the baton to Christian

Malcolm on the third leg, the top four teams in the field were comfortably ahead of their competitors. Four athletes from four different nations glided serenely in a line around the top bend as if synchronised. As Malcolm floated around the curve towards the home straight, Barbour left his starting mark, powering out exceptionally hard. He picked up his acceleration and drove his legs into the track to get up to top speed for the final straight sprint to qualification. But in getting out with such vigour, Barbour had left Malcolm with a lot to do with only a tiny window to exchange the baton in the permitted zone and the inevitable happened.

The baton hit the floor. Yet again, a line-up stacked full of talented individuals had been less than the sum of its parts. Despite the temptation to attribute blame on the individuals involved, you could not put this failure purely down to that one changeover.

People simply cannot be the best at things that they haven't done before. Barbour was new to the squad with no experience of world standard races. This was not a new skill for him; he had taken part in numerous relays before and conducted countless practices; but this was an entirely new experience for him. He had not shouldered this level of scrutiny and pressure before. The tightrope he was walking wasn't three feet off the ground. It was three hundred feet. He had never felt the knife-edge nerves at the top of the home straight as a flock of the world's fastest humans flew towards him. He would never have felt so anxious or borne such a weight of responsibility to deliver with so much at stake. Even the ability to judge his own acceleration against that of an athlete recently in a World Championship final coming towards him while also exchanging a baton was new. This scenario provided a young, inexperienced athlete a very foreign flood of information at the precise moment where he needed to execute the calmness of thought to trust all aspects of team training.

Pressure can be a catalyst for success or for failure in sport. It can lead to a deep focus or to emotion overriding logic. Coping and thriving in these moments improves the more you immerse yourself in such situations. This is what experience is.

To attribute this error entirely to the pressure situation and an inexperienced team member papered over the cracks of a wider issue. The relay had for years been viewed by the athletes themselves as a bonus event, something of a bolt-on to their individual exploits. It was even regarded by some as a bit of fun. There was a high level of technical detail to impart in not a lot of time once a team had been selected. Coaches often put athletes in unfamiliar scenarios in order to cater for the worst possible situation but there was a chasm to be leapt between simulating this in training and the experience of the athlete in a 'live' setting. GB ice skating legends Torvill and Dean practised for five hours a day, for months on end, to synchronise their timings and movements for a competitive performance. Were the timings and synchronicity of a relay team as intricate and dependent on mutual understanding as theirs? Probably not, but the accuracy and speed of the skill to be executed certainly was. Given they were rivals rather than training partners, even finding time to practise was an issue. When they did manage it, there was an air of detachment rather than cooperation. Prior to the Sydney Olympics, Darren and Jason's relationship became rockier as they both realised how much of a threat they were to one another's dreams. Instead of embraces there came smiles, then merely acknowledgement between them.

Expecting a relay team to come together as fast as they could run was clearly incorrect and the idea that chucking the four speediest athletes together on the track while ignoring concepts like team dynamics, cohesion and purpose could be successful was evidently a bust. Frank Dick, a former UK Athletics administrator and coach, diplomatically stated in the press that, "We need to give athletes what they need to achieve, not what they want. There is a big difference."

Even from his distant vantage point, Dick was close to the mark. The relay team had, up until the turn of the millennium, been an athlete-led enterprise. This would have been great had the attitude been one of excellence driven from within. More often than not it was an environment where superstar athletes controlled the narrative and set the tone with individual events deemed more important.

Analysing the simple logistics behind preparing a relay quartet yields surprising results. If only four athletes were selected for a relay squad – i.e. the bare minimum to compete - a coach could still select up to twenty-four different combinations when it came to the running order. From 1999 to 2002, no fewer than nine athletes ran consistently for the British relay team:

Jason Gardener. Darren Campbell. Allyn Condon. Dwain Chambers. Iain Mackie. Marlon Devonish. John Barbour. Mark Lewis-Francis. Christian Malcolm.

Choosing four athletes from a pool of nine with four different potential positions in the order meant there were no fewer than three thousand and twenty-four different possible permutations. Good for the notion of strength in depth, bad for the notions of familiarisation and consistency with techniques and timings. Britain had plenty of the former but recent evidence showed that it badly needed the latter.

> "British Athletics wasn't awash with sub-10 second 100m athletes like the Americans or the Jamaicans had, or in those days the Canadians too. In fact, even in Europe you had

> France bringing through some world-class sprinters. A well-drilled British team, familiar with one another, and tight, was the only way we could compete."
>
> — Darren Campbell

It felt as if Edmonton was just the latest lapse born from a culture of low-continuity in the British relay team. Members were perpetually being asked to chop and change but maintain a team bond with one another. There were ten athletes selected for the wider relay squad in Sydney, all vying for four places with the end result of that altogether too painful. Jayne Torvill and Christopher Dean trained with one another. They didn't train separately only to reintroduce their partnership come competition time.

A year after Sydney in Edmonton, was the new addition on the anchor leg John Barbour familiar with his new teammates? Had they all run at World Championships before? Had their relay transition skills been tested under immense pressure? Did they have an innate knowledge of their own behaviours and habits as a team? Did the team have the ability to have honest conversations with one another on how everyone was feeling? Could they discuss the various interpersonal variables they felt would contribute towards successfully getting the baton around? Did they have subconscious faith in one another?

The answer to each is no.

With the USA's winning position at the Edmonton games being annulled in 2005 due to Tim Montgomery's drug suspension, South Africa became World Champions with a time of 38.47. This was the slowest time for a gold medal relay team in a World Championships or Olympic Games since 1964. Why is that significant? The 1964 Tokyo Olympic games were run on an old-fashioned cinder track, before synthetic tracks were introduced in Mexico City in 1968.

This wasn't just an opportunity. This had been an open goal for the British team to win World Championships gold. They had absolutely blown it.

8

MARLON DEVONISH

"There was a football match involving Clifford Bridge Primary when I was about nine years old. Dad came to watch me and since he rarely did this, I was apprehensive as well as excited. While in the middle of the game, I could see my dad pacing the sidelines talking to himself, not really watching me. I was in the game but became consumed by watching my dad not watching me.

Suddenly the ball came my way and it got intercepted because I was distracted, and it resulted in a goal for the opposition. My team-mates immediately were like, "Marlon man, what are you doing?" I loved my dad more than anything else in the world but at times I got embarrassed, at other times I got a little angry. In time I learned to accept that dad wasn't the problem – it was the illness."

— Marlon Devonish

Desmond Devonish was a welder by profession. His proficiency and strength with his hands helped him be not only a very good welder but a karate black belt as well. No one was ever going to challenge his word or authority within the household. Marlon took discipline and a competitive instinct from his dad and work ethic and persistence from his mum. Vivian Devonish worked as a nurse in the NHS for 43 years. She often worked nights, returning home in the early hours to help prepare Marlon and the twins, Anthony and Cheryl, to start their day before getting some well-deserved sleep. The Devonishs weren't a poor family but luxuries were thin on the ground. Hard work wasn't an option.

Desmond had grown up in Barbados a smart and articulate child, both academic and sporty in nature. He was adept enough at mathematics for his school teacher to whisper to him that there was no point in him being there, since there was nothing the staff could teach him in the language of algebra and trigonometry that he didn't already know. With mum Vivian fulfilling her calling in nursing and uncle John the academic scientist, there were plenty of positive role models in Marlon's family. He had a very happy upbringing where he felt safe and secure, surrounded by people who were making something of themselves.

When Marlon was around eight, Desmond started to have mental health issues which worsened over a long period of time. This smart, fit individual, respected as a family man at home and a diligent professional at work, showed signs of slowing down. The prevailing attitude at the time was that mental health trouble was a sign of weakness and Desmond could never find the right balance between accepting the reasons to take medication and refusing his need to take it, caught between pride and pragmatism. Here was an intelligent individual who thrived on the discipline and rigour of his skilled work and of martial arts, under siege from the chaotic and relentless nature of a mental illness.

Desmond - who would sadly pass away in the winter of 2020 - was diagnosed with severe depression and vascular dementia. This loving, caring father became shrouded in a cloak of anxiety and withdrawal from the world, cruelly depriving the Devonish family of his personality. The conversations that Marlon wanted to have with his dad about girls, football, music and school all became impossible as discussions endlessly drew on events from thirty years in the past. He looked up to his dad and had loved spending time with him, but as Desmond's condition became more and more prohibitive. Marlon realised that he was not going to be able to rely on his father to look after him and the family.

Clifford Bridge Primary School was about a ten minute walk from the family home in Binley. Marlon began running home to cut that ten minutes down and as that commute got quicker and quicker, he began to think he might have an aptitude for running. He had less aptitude for academic work, making jokes in class to compensate, and his relationships with his teachers didn't go further than mutual tolerance. The school had a system of point scoring, with the reward of being allowed to go swimming at the end of the week. Most of Marlon's class enjoyed a weekly dip but since Marlon was in the deep end academically, he rarely found himself even in the shallow end of the pool. Caludon Castle High School was where Marlon discovered his creative streak as well as developing his increasingly evident sporting talents, later exhibiting artwork at the Windsor Contemporary Art Fair. Two teachers, Mr Coleman & Miss Ryan, could see that he had a talent for sprinting and recommended he go down to Kirby Corner track - home of Coventry Godiva Harriers Athletic Club - to meet with the coaches. Here he met Wayne Morant.

Morant was a coach-athlete. The training group held him in high regard as unlike most other coaches, he was applying the same rigorous regime to himself that he coached to his group. He was walking his talk. Morant could see that Marlon was raw and had realistic athletic aspirations but that there was no direction or method in his slightly unorthodox gait. Anything Wayne was learning he immediately taught to Marlon. Being a young coach, he was learning up-to-the-minute techniques and paradigms which he could immediately test on himself and impart to his pupil. It also meant that Marlon had an inside look at coaching methodologies and an unusually active role in his own development. They knew they needed to work hard on Marlon's technique and the fast feedback loop they engendered between them was unquestionably one of the reasons why Devonish became such a technically consistent runner.

TEENAGE MARLON WOULD FEEL MOST COMFORTABLE LISTENING to A Tribe Called Quest and Snoop Doggy Dogg with his cousins Steve, Andrew and Mark, at their respective houses. The four of them would listen for hours, taking breaks to mix vinyl on decks and recording their efforts on cassette tapes. They loved the musicality and rhythm of the increasingly popular gangsta rap genre but Marlon was fondest of the storytelling. He listened incessantly to Redman, Lords of the Underground and Dr. Dre, adored Hip Hop and R&B and seeing his friend Brendan's uncle working as a DJ in Nuneaton, Marlon could imagine making his passion more than just an interest. Music was huge for Marlon.

Desmond Devonish continued to drop his son at the track but his mental illness was worsening and he couldn't hang around and wait for Marlon to finish meaning that after training with the Godiva athletes until nightfall, Marlon would usually walk the two hours home. He would stroll along Kirby Corner road, listening to mixtapes he had concocted with his cousins over and over until either the Walkman batteries ran out or he arrived home. This long, regular walk emphasised that Marlon's dad was increasingly unable to fend for him and although he was still the class clown at school, his dad's illness was demonstrating the need for him to grow up. He also wanted to help his mother and for her to be proud of him. To alleviate the various pressures on her, he wouldn't have needed to look very far in order to find some nefarious way of making a fast living, but this simply was not in his make-up. He didn't want to be the one in the family that was causing drama, instead deciding to grow up and become the man of the house while he was still a boy.

> "Your independence can be given, shown, or forced upon you. I experienced all three."
>
> — Marlon Devonish

Being in the early stages of his coaching career, Wayne was asking questions as much as he was instructing. He and Marlon were unusually honest with each other as they stumbled around in the dark somewhat to begin with, bringing in close friend and training partner Brendon Ghent to join in with their discussions. Morant was a thoughtful, caring and authentic coach and in their environment of no pretence, Marlon knew his coach's journey as much as the coach knew his.

> "I felt that Wayne always considered my opinions and asked my thoughts on things. We were planning training together and I felt hugely invested in my own development because of it."

— Marlon Devonish

A positive by-product of being coached by someone who was constantly absorbing and applying new information was in the process itself. For instance, when Wayne was learning about athlete-centred initiatives, he would involve Marlon in his own schedule building, ensuring his athlete felt he had ownership and responsibility over the sessions. Marlon wanted to know what they were doing and why they were doing it and Wayne had to have good reasons ready. This dynamic spurred each of them to continuously do better and Marlon's performances improved in leaps and bounds.

This became a problem.

Marlon's improvements meant that he was competing at an increasingly high level. He needed the level of his training sessions to be as close to his competitive environment as possible. This wasn't happening at Coventry where he was now well out in front. To improve further, Marlon needed to train with people who would force him onto a higher plane of performance. After a senior meet with the British team, Marlon had a conversation with Mark Richardson, one of Britain's main 400m runners, who confided in Marlon that he needed to work on his speed. Marlon reciprocated by stating he needed to work with someone who would test him in training and through one athlete's honesty with another, the next stage in Marlon's development had revealed itself.

Back in Coventry, Wayne fully understood, being mature and understanding enough to appreciate the positive situation that he had helped to create. Marlon went to west London to train with Tony Lester's group which aside from Richardson, included stellar names such as Roger Black, Abi Oyepitan, Marcia Richardson, Mark Hylton, Tim Benjamin and later Chris Lambert. Marlon had wanted a higher level of competition in training and he was about to get more than he bargained for.

In Coventry, Marlon had been training with athletes looking to break into regional competitions whereas now he was competing daily against a group of national winners overseen by a proven and successful coach. He thrived under Tony Lester, a man who prioritised respect and created a no nonsense culture of hard work informed by his previous life in the Army. Wayne and Marlon had been learning and growing together but here the seniority was clear. Devonish was trying to become successful whereas Lester already was. Marlon needed to earn his stripes.

Wayne Morant had been a fantastic technical coach for Marlon but Tony Lester had a precious familiarity with knowing what it took to win. He paired Marlon with Mark Richardson, challenged him to work on his speed endurance and let them go at each other. They battled ferociously on the training track but became close enough to laugh about it on the way home. All they did was train, eat and sleep, enabled by a grant from Sport England and funding from wealthy benefactor and athletics fan, the late Eddie Kulikundis who sadly died in 2021.

The two athletes became firm friends. Mark made Marlon feel welcome, driving him around and taking him under his wing while Thames Valley Athletics quickly became a place he felt comfortable. Marlon's mother made it clear to him that he would always be able to come home if needs be so he could take some risks and push towards his goals without having to worry about having a landing spot if things went wrong.

Having consigned the mess of the 2000 Olympic relay performance to history, 2001 was shaping up to be a good year. Training was going well and Marlon's performances were improving. He took a huge step forward by becoming British champion in the 200m, defeating Christian Malcolm and Dwain Chambers, with training partner Mark Richardson winning the 400m title. He would go to the worlds in Edmonton as one of the preeminent athletes in his event.

The world leader in that event was the Greek Hercules Konstantinos Kenteris, who had overtaken Darren Campbell in the closing stages of Men's 200m at the Sydney Olympics the previous year. Kenteris was a constant for Marlon in Edmonton. They were drawn in the same heat, in the same quarter-final, in the same semi-final and together in the final. Kenteris enjoyed a phenomenal three years between 2000-2003 before disappearing in a cloud of controversy, uncertainty and confusion at his home Olympic Games, vanishing from the public eye almost as quickly as he had appeared. He was hard to escape for Campbell in 2000 and for Devonish in 2001, his presence looming over other world class athletes. In the 200m final Kenteris was trailing the field in last as they rounded the bend into the home straight, but finding an extra spurt of speed and energy, he pulled away from the field to win in a similar style to his Olympic victory. Marlon was one of a straight line of runners that saw Kenteris pull away, and ultimately could not make amends when the relay team faltered in the semi-final.

Consistency at the highest level was bound to bring rewards in time but the failure for this consistency to be transferred to the relay team became a stone in his shoe. He was an established relay runner, yet this supposed source of medal glory for him and the British team coughed and spluttered its way from one championship to the next. This new wave of British sprinters, belying their hard-charging alpha male personas, showed evidence time and again of having a tendency to hesitate under pressure. The accusations of stage fright under the stress of a big occasion became inevitable. Whether addressing experienced relay runners like Marlon or first-timers like John Barbour, the reason for the failure of the British relay team was a lot more complex than simply the occasion being too much or some weakness in the team's DNA.

Marlon had been a regular fixture in the British Athletics team since 1997, not missing a single event, and there was clearly something missing when it came to the relay. As an ever-present, he was in a strong position to make a judgment, but the truth was even he wasn't sure what the problem was.

Commentators, coaches and peers all had their opinions. Arrogance said some. Immaturity, others. Poor execution was the symptom but what was the cause? Even with his longevity, Marlon had only been involved in twelve relay teams, a sample size that was probably too small and contained too little information to yield the one golden answer. One constant aspect was that the components of the team were never as strong as the strongest teams in other nations. Britain didn't have a continual production line of sub-ten-second 100m runners like the USA and later, Jamaica, had. The changeovers of the batons therefore needed to take a much higher priority since this was an area where precious milliseconds could be gained or lost. The changeovers demanded synchronicity between two people, a harmony and strong dynamic between the individuals concerned. An emotional connection, even as base-level as respecting and liking one another as teammates, was as important as the statistics and times. Trust is uncoachable. It has to be developed and nurtured. A high-performance team needed to be grown, not simply assembled.

Whatever the reason or hypothesis, however you parsed the data or debated the merits of the individual athletes, it was obvious to the naked eye that there was an undeniable lack of cohesion. They just weren't a team.

> "You have to be more in-tune with one another than you'd think to get that baton around the track at that speed. Handing and receiving the baton at that speed is a skill. That's why I preferred the last leg so I didn't have to do it!"
>
> — Mark Lewis-Francis

Why does a team drop a baton?

The task seems simple, a failure to manage it infuriating. But when you break down what's actually happening, the logistics are simple yet surprising. The athletes run away from one another at speeds of over eleven metres per second. That's the length of three cars per second. The space that is allocated to exchange the baton is only 20m long, with athletes allowed to run for 10m prior to the exchange zone to build up their acceleration (and to avoid a seismic collision as one athlete hits a static team-mate at high speed). The bottom line is that two athletes both travelling at around 25mph have approximately 0.8 seconds to exchange the baton cleanly. This presumes that they have matched their synchronicity to ensure one doesn't run away without having been given the baton in the first place. Nought point eight seconds. This matching merely ensures that the baton gets around successfully – there is no margin shaving involved in that calculation to steal a march on the other teams. That comes later.

Consider the physical perspective. One athlete is inevitably tiring as they approach another who is exploding away at full power. To ensure smoothness of transition, the outgoing runner needs to be traveling close to top speed with the baton changed as late as possible. This means that the best place to exchange the baton is often at the end of the legal zone to allow the outgoing runner to get up to speed. While the speed of the runners vary, the velocity of the baton needs to remain both consistent and as high as possible.

> "It's the speed of the baton that wins the race, not the speed of the sprinters."
>
> — Marlon Devonish

From the psychological perspective, the athletes keeping calm, feeling familiar and safe with one another and avoiding indecision ensures that the physical act can be performed as best it can. There are so many moving parts, so many rapidly changing angles, speeds and distances that you are almost inviting failure by selecting inexperience. Handing a rookie a relay spot at a major championships with little practice is almost planning for a calamity.

Relay athletes needed to be comfortable with one another, to have an innate knowledge of one another's idiosyncrasies and to be able to call out arrogance and overconfidence if it reared its head. If you didn't really trust one another, how could you ever really help each other push the limits that needed to be pushed to win a medal?

Athletes needed to know their teammates inside out and often that came from making mistakes and then appraising them with often brutal honesty. Yet in his time as a member of the relay team, Marlon had seen a culture of accepting mistakes, of tolerating tardiness and a lack of rigour. Without a continuity of membership, with athletes regularly coming in and out of the team, many chose silence and lip-biting over constructive confrontation in a misguided effort to maintain team harmony. While perhaps well-intentioned, this left a hollow core where the spirit of the team should have been.

The concept of a squad of six equals, with no identified leadership or guidance, immediately lent itself to a clouding of responsibilities. It practically invited the squeakiest gates to have all of the oil. The coaches held the reins with regards to strategy and selection but were often overshadowed by strong personalities when they had to be custodians and police what behaviours were tolerated. There was also an unwitting clash of cultures, the differing backgrounds of the athletes and coaches causing a natural distrust of those in senior positions. At school, Marlon Devonish was told he wasn't capable of certain things while in Bath, Jason Gardener endured a racist teacher and struggled to fit in. Darren Campbell and Mark Lewis-Francis had been decade-long rebels against academic authority figures at their respective institutions, with Mark having been excluded twice. GB relay team coach Steve Perks was a school headteacher by profession. The demographics could not have been planned any worse.

From this dysfunctional environment sprung the seeds of future success. Steve Perks had his work cut out, and to his credit, he gained the athletes' trust through his diligence and knowledge. His big challenge was to get the athletes to embrace honesty and integrity as a foundation for teamwork. This meant accepting weaknesses to identify potential breaks in the chain. Amongst ego-fuelled athletes that spent their entire lives competing with each other, this was a foreign concept. Not an inch was given, displays of confidence were the norm and one could easily see how broaching the subject of needing to practice until skills were mastered could be perceived as showing your enemies the chink in your armour. Athletes in this environment needed the oxygen of self-assuredness to survive. Having the honesty to admit uncertainties and issues would be pounced upon.

The British relay team had developed a subservience to athlete confidence and conviction. This team kept telling itself that it had no weaknesses, was one of the best in the world and that if things didn't go as they planned it would be down to an 'event' or 'bad luck' or 'inexperience'. It was never anyone's fault and it certainly wasn't because they weren't particularly good at the seemingly simple skill of getting a baton around the track. Coaches, commentators and fellow athletes all kept pressing the same message of "believe in yourself, have confidence, do things with conviction" to the extent that accepting the presence of any weakness or a mistake became anathema. Accepted wisdom was that if this team displayed confidence and assertion in its ability, it would unlock success. This was the complete opposite to what it truly needed. The solution required introspection, humility and the ability to analyse weaknesses.

The problem was encapsulated in the athletes' reaction to failure on the big stage. They truly didn't know what was to blame when things went awry, their bemused, puzzled faces at baton drops not staged for the cameras. They didn't know the cause of the mishaps but each individual knew that they couldn't possibly be to blame. With so many personnel involved, so many talkers and not enough walkers, as a collective unit they hadn't made enough mistakes in practice to prevent them happening when the world was watching.

MARLON DEVONISH WAS UNACQUAINTED WITH THE PRINCIPLES and precedents involved in historic sporting triumphs as a young athlete but the more he participated in relay squad successes and failures, the more he became convinced of the necessity of learning and applying the lessons of the past. He didn't just want to know what lay behind underperformance, he needed to. Each failure was costing him medals.

He wasn't yet in a position to lead but he came to realise that having the ability to lead as well as being able to be led underpinned high-performing teams. People needed to be able to instruct as well as take instruction, to ask for advice as well as give it. This meant that the personalities involved needed to be the type that would comfortably allow this freedom of expression to exist. With his father's mental illness having placed him in an unfamiliar and difficult situation years earlier, Marlon had proven himself to be adaptable and mature enough to change. He had assumed the role within the family of being dependable, robust, and reliable, without being asked.

He knew exactly what the relay squad required. He'd done it before.

9

2 YEARS TO GO
MANCHESTER & MUNICH 2002

> "I was going through a really bad stage. I was injured. I was separated from my partner. My ambition and drive had gone. Then I went to this run and saw people lining the streets at midnight in the rain, and a smile slowly started to return to my face and my love for the sport kind of grew again from there."
>
> — Darren Campbell

The town of Mountain Ash in South Wales was an unlikely place for Darren Campbell to rediscover his love for athletics. The previous year had been horrible, both professionally and personally, and at midnight in a rain-soaked craggy town overlooking a cold Welsh valley, you'd be forgiven for thinking his annus horribilis wasn't a one off.

The town's *Nôs Galan* races were an annual celebration of local running hero Guto Nyth Brân and a mystery runner was invited to take part in the race every year. Jamie Baulch,

Christian Malcolm and Iwan Thomas had all participated in previous years, and in 2001, Darren was invited to be the guest of honour. In truth, he felt a million miles from the Olympic silver medallist of a year before and that it was disingenuous of him to attend an event where hundreds would take part for the love of running. He had fallen out of love with the sport a few times previously and this time could have been the last.

Seeing the smiling faces running for pure pleasure in the middle of an icy night in the Welsh valleys, he had a change of heart and drove home with a clearer mind. The Commonwealth Games were in his home city of Manchester in seven months time and he realised that he was exceptionally fortunate to be considered one of the world's elite athletes. The cold rain and darkness of Mountain Ash had given him a little prod. The problem was that despite this change of heart, he was still injured, out of shape and untrained. Months of apathy meant he was miles behind where he needed to be to medal in Manchester.

TRAVELLING TO COMPETE IS A SOULLESS AND CHASTENING existence for most athletes. Nondescript hotels, budget flights and competition villages with facilities designed and built by the cheapest, cost-cutting bidder. Edmonton had been a prime example of how sterile these places could be, with no atmosphere, no vibes and nothing much to do. Some of the customs and procedures on the European circuit, even ranging down to the food and who you shared a room with, were haphazard and nerve-inducing. The Manchester Commonwealth Games was different for the English athletes given that they would be familiar with everything. Food, travel, the hotels, the entertainment options, the language and even the brand new stadium. This was a massive boost.

Marlon Devonish shared a room with Mark Hylton at the Commonwealths. This was a fillip, given that both athletes not only respected one another, but were close friends. Marlon and Mark together made it feel like they were at home. Things felt natural and comfortable and Marlon was in good form, winning the Commonwealth Games 200m trials in a record time of 20.18.

Form or no form, the Commonwealth Games always had an ace up its sleeve when it came to the sprint events. Some of the powerhouses such as Canada and Jamaica would be in attendance and predicting what talent would arrive from around the world was a lottery. The 100m final brought together Jason Gardener, Mark Lewis-Francis and Dwain Chambers, all representing England, against world stars Kim Collins and Deji Aliu. All three Englishmen were to be left disappointed, not only with their placings, but with their performances. Jason and Mark were in the mix for the medals at 60m but Jason wanted it so badly, he tensed up into a ball of muscle and it didn't happen for him. Mark went one better, tearing his hamstring thirty metres out from the finish line, ending his race and his games. Mark had been close to Collins in the middle lane but he spent the last fifteen strides attempting to slow down on only one leg, the other totally useless to him.

Gardener's struggles over 100m were clear evidence of an athlete still learning to master the event and the balancing act of performing three or four times in two days at major championships. His strength was his phenomenal start, always getting out of the blocks quickly, but he could never fully relax and go through the gears. He would think too much and too hard, never arriving at the point of doing things subconsciously and flowing naturally towards the end of the race. He had his foot down on the accelerator in 4th gear, grinding it out instead of moving into 6th and running more efficiently.

Of all the countries to fall under the umbrella of the former British Commonwealth, it was the small island of St Kitts and Nevis who provided the winner in Kim Collins, an athlete that when it came to size, was almost as diminutive as his home country.

> "Do it for Manchester, Darren!"
>
> — A voice in the crowd prior to the 200m final

Marlon Devonish and Darren Campbell had qualified for the final of the 200m. Marlon knew how pumped Darren would be on home turf in Manchester, but he didn't fully appreciate the depth of emotion and determination that powered Campbell that day. All the athletes knew that he had a propensity to produce better performances in the big events, but the Darren Campbell that took to the blocks in the 200m final had just come through a year of personal turmoil and was not the conditioned athlete that had won Olympic silver. Marlon had purposefully under-run in the earlier rounds to conserve energy for the final whereas Darren had been maxing out merely to get to the start line. The Welshman Christian Malcolm had also qualified for the 200m, highlighting the burgeoning strength in depth of UK sprinting.

Devonish was drawn outside one of the world's greatest ever athletes in Frankie Fredericks of Namibia. This was hardly ideal for Marlon as he would in effect be running blind, unable to see a likely medal contender until later in the race. His attitude was that he would simply have to make Fredericks come and get him, his belief backed by the press who had suggested in print that the Namibian wasn't a particularly strong bend runner. Once the gun went, Fredericks was utterly determined to make his detractors eat their words. He flew past the field on the first bend, only Campbell and Devonish providing any company whatsoever as they hit the home straight. Fredericks cruised through the gears, his technique perfectly relaxed. Marlon drove hard to catch his English teammate Campbell who was defying all expectations and over-producing in a final once again. As they crossed the line, Devonish dipped and pipped Campbell to take silver with Fredericks winning gold. Marlon had won a highly creditable silver with consistent performances through the rounds while Darren had proved to himself that he could win medals and find a performance in even the most unlikely circumstances.

The way the British athletes won these medals, Devonish leaning on his technical proficiency and strategic approach, the passionate Campbell clawing his way up the track, would be telling in retrospect. The two played to their strengths both in the final and in the build up and were rewarded with places on the rostrum.

The relay final was to be an unofficial trial for the British athletes as the usual team was fractured into its constituent national parts. The English team had a stellar squad to choose from with Devonish, Campbell, Gardener, Condon, Lewis-Francis and Chambers all present at the Games. Even though the latter two had retired injured in the 100m final, there was still a strong quartet available to run. Christian Malcolm represented Wales in the final, while the various other teams contained world-class athletes such as Asafa Powell, Marc Burns, Bruny Surin, and Michael Frater.

There was a notable solidarity and positive vibe emanating from the English team where coach Clarence Callendar had allowed the athletes some expression and decision making responsibilities within a disciplined framework. The athletes were a little tired but clearly motivated and happy. There was an extra sense of fun and opportunity in performing for a wildly vocal and passionate Manchester crowd, who cheered on local hero Darren Campbell running the anchor leg. A close race saw England and Jamaica cross the line together, the outstretched chest of Campbell fending off Asafa Powell for gold.

As the partisan crowd roared for their heroes, the team couldn't help but smile on their lap of honour. Gardener, Devonish, Condon and Campbell had managed the weight of expectation and could now enjoy the moment. The exchanges and timings were by no means perfect and the injury-interrupted build-up far from ideal, but the reception they received from the roaring crowd spoke volumes. Feeding off each other's energy had led to a gold medal and made for a very good feeling indeed.

Immediately after the Commonwealth Games, Jason Gardener decided to change coaching group, joining Malcolm Arnold's group in Bath. He'd been flip flopping between Arnold's group, which included Colin Jackson and Jamie Baulch, and his usual coach Dave Lease in Cardiff prior to the Commonwealth Games. Jason and Dave's relationship had been straining under the pressure of increased expectation with fun and progress increasingly absent in their professional arrangement. This had been exacerbated by Jason wallowing in self-pity during the 2001 season where he had been affected by injury and a lack of impetus. He was also wondering why his training regime looked so markedly different to everyone else's. He was an athlete with a phenomenal strength to weight ratio, able to comfortably lift over double his bodyweight in myriad exercises but he only ran on the track once or twice per week, contrasting hugely with what his competitors were doing.

This regime had yielded incredible results for Jason, placing him second only to Linford Christie in the British quickest 100m all-time list, but he made the decision to try something new. He switched to Arnold's group and while a change was as good as a rest at first, Jason could not resist the pull of returning to Lease where he felt more natural. Upon returning though, both realised things had changed and that the time really had come. Jason and Dave parted on good terms for a final time.

> "If you are going to be with us what are you going to bring?"
>
> — Malcolm Arnold

Arnold was widely acknowledged as being one of the world's finest track and field coaches and he held court in Gardener's home city of Bath. Arnold was also known for being ruthless and pragmatic when it came to adopting new athletes, coaches or support staff, refusing to accept passivity or someone that wouldn't add something to his group. Ego-driven and often selfish athletes were thus forced to be constructive and to actively give to others if they wanted the benefits of his training.

It seemed the wisest move for Gardener. He got to go home to Bath, to test himself with someone new and to put the past year or so behind him. Emotionally, strategically and logistically it made sense. These qualities were important to Jason, playing a decisive role in his career way before lining up for one of Arnold's sessions. It involved a practice camp at Annecy prior to the Munich European Championships in 2002, held a few weeks after the Manchester Commonwealth Games.

Athletes' salaries are like everyone else's. The money they receive is judged on their market value for the most part but, of course, it comes down to how much someone is willing to pay for their services. Your perceived market value and what someone is willing to pay are not always the same figure.

Despite any concerns about the level of remuneration a Premiership footballer receives compared to someone like a doctor, the fact remains that even if the salary clock was set back to zero for both occupations, it would not take too much time for the commercial might of football to return back the current status quo. Talking about the worth and value of a sportsperson in financial terms is a never-ending argument with no solution and probably no correct answer.

This is different to arguing what a sportsperson is paid for and particularly in the modern era, what an athlete provides an employer reaches far beyond the field of play. Merchandising, ambassadorial roles or co-opting an athlete's individual following all come into play here, meaning that there are further rewards on offer for those that play ball off the pitch.

From a philosophical perspective, being a 'good pro' means different things to different people. In some ways, Diego Maradona was the ultimate professional for S.S.C. Napoli and Argentina. He delivered titles and a World Cup in a style befitting the romantic game, doing what he was being paid for on the field. However, with respect to his off-field escapades and controversies, many would not consider him a 'good professional', despite him delivering exactly what his profession demanded of him.

For most people, 'professionalism' within sport denotes a dedication to constant improvement, an ascetic lifestyle, the idea of always looking to get better, to push the limits of performance. Professionals in this respect get paid to live every minute of their lives in a way that does not compromise their performance or their quest for success. Everything from the journeys they take, the amount of sleep they have, the food they eat, the company they keep, professionalism lends itself to a notion of being paid to live a highly restrictive lifestyle. There is no sport like track and field, where everything is measured in thousandths of a second, which can lay claim to being as exposing or restrictive. Life is ruthlessly monastic. A late night means an added tenth of a second. While most of us get to put our work down and pick up a beer to relax, athletes are on the clock every minute of their lives. There is no switching off when Olympic medals are at stake.

Athletes are athletes but they're also people. Everyone is different and ought to be treated differently. Having said that, within a team what is tolerated and not tolerated needs to be crystal clear, otherwise people can and will take liberties. Whether cloaked in a progressive model of individualisation or an athlete-centred focus, people doing whatever the hell they wanted was happening with wild abandon within the British relay team at the turn of the millennium. This wasn't Phil Jackson allowing Dennis Rodman to go to Las Vegas to blow off steam or Sir Alex Ferguson navigating around Eric Cantona's kung-fu kick and subsequent meanderings. UK track athletes were under no obligation to abide by team standards and faced no repercussions if they breached them. It was messy and amateurish. This notion wasn't challenged by anyone, simply being the modus operandi at the time and for Jason Gardener, it would precipitate a parting of the ways.

Relay practices were scheduled within the season by UK Athletics coaches. If athletes were selected as part of a wider sprint squad, they were invited and expected to attend. One such meeting, to organise the logistics and scheduling of practices, occurred in a London Heathrow Airport hotel at the end of winter, with ten of Britain's leading sprinters in attendance. Athletes had travelled from all over the British Isles, the longer journeys being taken by Ian Mackie from Scotland and Allyn Condon from Liverpool. Despite their long commutes, they were at the meeting on time.

The same respect was not shown by everyone. Three of the sprinters were late, ironically the ones based closest to the location of the meeting. The others waited. One hour turned into two, but there was still no sign of the tardy trio. When they eventually sauntered into the hotel lobby over two hours late, all three were conspicuously tucking into a McDonald's.

The other athletes were furious. The precarious harmony of the relay squad at that time relied on everyone keeping their cool, sitting on their hands and saying nothing. The abundance of talent and the lack of direction from above meant that speaking out or causing a fuss was liable to get you cast out of the squad rather than leading to improved behavioural standards. The tone was set from above and this behaviour going unsanctioned by the coaches set the other athletes' teeth on edge. When the trio were selected for the squad, any remaining respect for the coaches and the environment dissipated completely.

Unbeknown to the athletes, the coaches had decided to deal with the situation privately by having a word with the guilty parties afterwards, but the perception to the wider group was these guys had taken liberties and got away with it. As the transgressors never admitted to having been spoken to, the perception was that a lack of professionalism and even insolence towards the team were being glossed over. Addressing the issue in public would have gone a long way to maintaining a degree of team spirit, if only to reinforce that discipline was non-negotiable.

Whether by design or not, allowing such behaviour by a select few privileged them over the other athletes. It was a truly dreadful way of moulding a team and this was not an isolated incident. The same athletes later turned up over ninety minutes late to a sanctioned British Athletics relay meeting, arriving in a helicopter after an Adidas photo-shoot. The rockstar optics of the helicopter arrival spoke volumes. There were athletes that felt superior to their contemporaries, that they were entitled to special treatment and that they didn't owe the group anything. Such incidents, despite creating momentary mirth and enjoyment, revealed a hierarchy that wasn't supposed to exist within the group. The helicopter was more of an exhibition of Adidas' financial might rather than the athletes' influence but it served to highlight that there was an attitude of doing something just to see if you could get away with it.

This lacklustre behaviour destroyed any prospect of engendering high operating standards within the group. How could one athlete call out another for mistiming a changeover if the team allowed two hours lateness to go unmentioned? If the athletes felt unable to speak up about what was and wasn't unacceptable, how would they be able to really drill down into the fine margins that decide Olympic finals? They couldn't even tell each other to turn up on time.

2 YEARS TO GO
ANNECY, FRANCE 2002

The beautiful city of Annecy on the French side of the Alps seemed a generous location for a training camp, but it was befitting the strap-line for British Athletics at the time for its athletes: 'No Compromise'.

Yet there were compromises at every turn. Athletes would travel in the cheapest economy seats on planes, commute on budget buses, stay at the cheapest hotels and often share rooms with athletes they didn't know. The Annecy training camp for Jason meant a 5am start from Bath, a two hour drive to Heathrow airport to arrive a mandatory two hours early for international flights. Then the two hour flight to Geneva in basic economy was followed by another two hour minibus journey to Annecy with a stop for lunch in a roadside cafe. This was how most tourists would travel to visit Annecy, so a tired and stiff-backed Jason felt that he shouldn't complain. That attitude changed sharply upon arrival when he was told to get ready as there would be a relay practice, right then.

> "Management knew I'd been suffering from sciatica for a while and it took me a long time to warm up and get ready to run. Training hard after a long travel day was a no-no."
>
> — Jason Gardener

He was incredulous. His sciatica would have been inflamed further by the journey but even if this wasn't the case, making a finely tuned athlete push himself after such a journey was risky. Stiffness and fatigue raised the likelihood of injury and with athletes judged on milliseconds, ignoring physiology and not adhering to best practices seemed foolhardy. For Jason, there was also an inherent risk in choosing not to run. Everyone around him was rising in the world rankings and he could ill afford any brake on his own progression, both in times or in his relationships with the decision makers.

This all seemed so amateurish. There's no possible way that someone with any knowledge of preparing elite athletes would think this course of action was a good idea and even if they did, why hadn't Jason been told that he'd be training on arrival in Annecy? It was reminiscent of the official running across a carpark to tell Darren Campbell he wouldn't be in the relay team after the British trials. Ad hoc, insensitive and poorly thought through.

Nevertheless, in keeping with the habits and cultures that existed at the time within the group, Jason bit his lip, mildly stated his protestations and warmed up ready for the session. He was a conscientious professional and he'd do what was asked of him.

The result was a torn hamstring. Jason was furious. He had spent all year focussed on personal and team success and had gotten injured due to a compromise at best and coaching negligence at worst. Then in Annecy came the coup de grâce. He was told he wouldn't be in the team moving forward.

Later in the season at the European Championships in Munich, Gardener performed badly in the 100m as he struggled to regain fitness following the injury sustained in Annecy. Sitting there watching his British rivals win medals hurt psychologically and tested his spirit. He spoke with team psychologist Dave Collins, stating that he wanted to return home immediately as he was not fit enough to be a part of the relay and actually didn't want to be a part of it. Despite not being able to affect the situation positively, Dave empathised greatly and understood his rationale. Jason felt he had often put the team ahead of his individual aspirations and now resented this. Any notion of keeping the peace evaporated. He didn't care if what he said next blackballed him. He had had enough of the shabbiness, of the tolerance of amateurish behaviour and what he regarded as the general incompetence of the setup.

Upon arriving home to Bath, he wrote a letter to the Chief Executive of UK Athletics David Moorcroft, explaining his actions. He outlined how he felt the system was biased, that some managerial behaviour at the coalface of the organisation was atrocious, that the behaviours were not only amateur but tolerated as such and all these were valid reasons why Britain would underperform again and wouldn't win Olympic gold. Jason wasn't finished. He also stated that if his integrity was called into question about the reasons for leaving Munich and departing the relay team, he would give a copy of the letter to the media. On this note, Jason Gardener left the UK relay team to prioritise resurrecting his 100m career.

There were no winners at the end of this. The British relay team had lost a member ideally suited to running the first leg, the coaches had lost a strong athlete to consider for future selection and Jason had lost out. This incident may have only created a small stir in the sports pages at the time but it was a warning shot across the bow for UK Athletics. The seeds of Jason's incident had been sown months earlier, behind computer screens and phone lines. The logistical planning of transport, the availability and exclusivity of track use and timetables, the training programs and treatment sessions were all hampered by cost and a 'that'll do' approach.

The approach did not fulfil the mission statement. While it's easy to show how the situation made it impossible for the athletes to improve and perform at their best possible level, it was equally a problem for the coaches.

Steve Perks was not a full time coach. He shared a similar experience to Jason, leaving work on Friday, travelling overnight, coaching world class athletes all weekend, then leaving on Sunday evenings and arriving back to start work in just a few hours time. This was the accepted reality of the situation for coaches and athletes, under the impression that this was always what they were going to get. The media, who were fed the line of 'no compromise', would then put even more pressure on the athletes to succeed under the impression that they had received absolutely everything they would need. Not so much.

Everywhere you looked, there were short cuts. From an administrative perspective, it was a lesson learnt in trying to do the right thing but not having the mechanisms in place in order to be able to achieve that. The sport was in a period of transition between amateur and professional. Steve Perks and the coaches were trying to professionalise the environment and the administrators were trying to give them what they needed but everyone was operating with one hand tied behind their back. Everyone wanted the same thing; the athletes to win on the track, but misaligned expectations and incentives meant that everyone was pulling in different directions.

A dedicated training camp in Annecy sounded like something a high performance team would do. That it was organised like a school skiing trip was neither here nor there to the administrators, who had little to no knowledge of what a sprinter needed to physically perform and train at their best. From Steve Perks' point of view, he had a couple of days with the athletes and couldn't afford to lose a day of training with them. Jason felt the pressure and the desire to train and do right by the team while also feeling that he had no one really looking out for his best interests.

Despite the slogans and the beautiful surroundings of Annecy, the processes of a high performance environment were simply not in place. The wheels had started to turn as far as intention but notions such as justifying spend, and giving responsibilities and resources to people and holding them accountable were a few years away.

Now we're accustomed to seeing sports teams research and implement everything from sleep habits to blue-lit planes and sensory deprivation tanks to cryotherapy chambers in a constant search for an edge. The attitude towards supplementary performance initiatives was miles away from this in 2002. The team were at a training facility in the Alps, with their coaches and had the time to train. That was all they needed as far as anyone was concerned.

Sport is a copycat business. Once word gets out that one team is doing something, another jumps on the same bandwagon. This is even encouraged by whoever their provider is, given that they're financially incentivised to get more customers. If one team is paying for GPS tracking devices, it behoves the provider to get another team on board. Once that becomes the norm, there is no way of getting an edge through this initiative. You need to find the next one.

Finding something new is an experiment and this is why operating on the cutting edge is so hard. It involves someone allocating substantial time and money to interventions that might not even work that well. It is often not the coaches or the scientists that allow huge leaps in performance interventions to occur; it's the capability of the purse-holders to be on the same page and possess the same drive to succeed as those advocating changes. There's no use having a hunch that some new technology will get you an edge if you can't convince your organisation to pay for it. If you don't and someone else implements it successfully, you're already behind the curve.

Back in 2002, the administrators had the imperative to use or lose their funding without having enough to really make the changes that high performance required. The result was a sub par environment. The funding, logistics and organisation to facilitate high performance from on high had not caught up with the intentions of those working on the ground.

THE *OLYMPIASTADION* AND ATHLETES' VILLAGE AT MUNICH WILL be forever etched into memory for all the wrong reasons. The stadium itself was built on the site of the former Oberwiesenfeld airport where in 1938, Neville Chamberlain met Adolf Hitler to collect the infamous piece of paper proclaiming 'peace in our time'. The athletes' village became a scene for a more visceral form of terrorism and bloodshed in 1972, with the horrors of the Israeli team massacre during the Olympic Games.

The site of the terrorist attack at Connollystraße 31 had since been consecrated as a memorial to the victims as well as puzzlingly being used as a guest house for an institute, making the atmosphere at the village eerie and macabre. Everyone knew what had happened there and athletes walking around the village felt an instant empathy and attachment to the victims. The rooms were newly painted white and felt cold, the prison-like atmosphere and chilling history denying the athletes any comfort.

Darren Campbell had travelled to Munich as the reigning European 100m champion as well as being an Olympic 200m silver medallist, but that professional resumè had might as well belonged to a different Darren. He had suffered a tumultuous two years with injury and personal problems. He had managed to drag himself through a personal quagmire of pain and physical limitations to get to the Commonwealth Games and with his objective and frank outlook on life, could still not believe how his patched-up, undertrained body managed to get a bronze and a gold at those Games. He had always known that he was a ruthless competitor but a softer side had manifested itself in Manchester. He had been overwhelmed by the level of support and solidarity he had received from his home Manchester crowd, to the extent that he felt there were fifty thousand family members cheering him on to medal. The experience at Manchester reignited the love he had for the sport of athletics and gave him a belief that he had an uncanny ability to become a competitively callous character when he was on the track. He never thought he was beaten and the only time he would ever give up on a race was after the finish line.

Darren and Dwain Chambers had qualified for the Men's 100m final, Jason Gardener narrowly missing out on qualification in his semi-final, and after many false starts the race got underway at the fifth time of asking. Chambers galloped home confidently in front of Portugal's Francis Obikwelu in second with Darren closing in quickly for the bronze. Marlon also claimed a strong bronze medal in the 200m, narrowly pipping fourth-placed compatriot Christian Malcolm for the podium place. Jason watched his now former teammates storm to gold in the relay, capping a wonderful year for Marlon, Darren and Dwain Chambers. It also brought a well-deserved gold to Christian Malcolm who up until that point had been a medal-less member of many winning squads. Yet befitting the site of Neville Chamberlain's proclamation to the world, betrayal and deception would soon rear their ugly heads.

10

DARREN CAMPBELL

> "As my sufferings mounted I soon realized that there were two ways in which I could respond to my situation - either to react with bitterness or seek to transform the suffering into a creative force. I decided to follow the latter course."
>
> — Dr. Martin Luther King, Jr.

The City of Manchester Stadium, home of the 2002 Commonwealth Games, lies about ten miles to the north east from where one of Darren Campbell's friends was shot and killed a decade earlier. The light grey exterior of what would become the Etihad Stadium perfectly matched the bland concrete greyness of the Sale Racecourse estate where Darren and Sophia Campbell grew up with their mum Marva. The sporting amphitheatre the likes of Vincent Kompany, Sergio Aguero and David Silva would call home was first and foremost built to be the base of the English Commonwealth Games team and Darren Campbell was one of many English athletes vying to perform there. Young Darren felt compelled to be an Olympic athlete having been inspired by Jesse Owens - with whom he shares a birthday - and Carl Lewis after his incredible feats at the Los Angeles Olympic Games in 1984, where he emulated Owens by winning 4 gold medals in the same events.

Darren's passion for athletics probably saved his life. He grew up on some of Britain's toughest streets during their toughest periods. Manchester wasn't nicknamed "Gunchester" lightly with drugs, guns, assaults, theft, racial tension, riots and murder commonplace in the 1980s and 1990s. Darren Grant, as he was then named, was a member of one of the many teenage gangs in the Sale Racecourse area. The sense of belonging and acceptance that came from being a part of a gang contrasted with the isolation and loneliness of being bullied and marginalised at Ashton-on-Mersey school in Sale, where young black men were few and far between. Darren gravitated towards others like him at school, partly due to their shared experience but also as a survival measure against the rampant racism and bullying prevalent in the corridors.

Darren struggled at school and school struggled with him. He had no interest in anything except for demonstrating ambivalence towards his teachers and earning money through selling dinner tickets with his friends. The only other pursuit that he was showing an interest in was athletics and following the Los Angeles Olympic Games, the teenaged Darren announced to anyone who would listen that he would be an Olympian. For this he was ridiculed, humiliated and put in his place, not by his fellow students, but by some of the teachers who said that such 'pipe dreams' led to a life of crime. Rather than seeing this as something worth encouraging in the young Darren, most saw fit to mock him.

Perhaps these teachers just saw what they were used to seeing. An angry young black kid who would doubtless follow the stream of others into the great river of crime and lawlessness that existed on the streets after dark. They drove young Darren further into his shell and he became even more resentful of those who stood at the front of his classes at school. Why on earth should he conform to their conduct and accept their aspirations for him when they were so unwilling to pay any respect to his?

He had finally found an avenue to express his energy, something to concentrate on and pour himself into and it was being rubbished by those that knew little of the burning passion that lay inside him. The teachers in question further marginalised a young marginalised kid and rendered any hope of resuscitating Darren Grant's interest in traditional education redundant.

> "Once I saw that my teacher's name was 'D.Law' it obviously made him, in our eyes, Denis Law despite the fact his name was Dave. He was already on a head-start to that effect as a teacher to any pupil who loved football."
>
> — Darren Campbell

Fortunately for Darren, there was one teacher who wouldn't accept his preordained fate. His anger and academic apathy met a brick wall by the name of Mr. Dave Law. True to his name, the law was laid down in this teacher's class, yet his reasonable demeanour and understanding with Darren penetrated the angry young Campbell's defences. He brokered a détente with Darren, supporting the young man's dreams on the one hand and demanding his application and focus on the other.

Dave Law saw an opportunity to teach where his colleagues saw one to ridicule and used Darren's dream as leverage to build a positive relationship between his sporting ambitions and his education. He didn't drive a wedge between school life and Darren's Olympic dreams, the existing narrative in Darren's head. He moulded them both together, showed how one could support the other and involved Darren in their successful pursuit. His approach was centred around supporting the dreams of his student, while demonstrating how those dreams could benefit from the guidance and education that school could provide.

As well as having noble aims, Dave Law was also a clever fellow. He involved Darren's mum Marva, becoming co-conspirators in a scheme where sport would be encouraged if academic performance merited it and removed if it wasn't. The carrot was used at school, the stick at home and it worked. Darren went from being a constant classroom menace to being relatively anonymous and discreet in lessons, with a commensurate and marked improvement in his grades. This change in persona didn't just alter his perception among the teachers, but created a self-fulfilling prophecy where it became no longer necessary to be at the bottom and at the back of the class at the same time.

The bullied, slightly scared young Darren also benefited from a sizeable growth spurt early in his teenage years. This not only accelerated his sporting development by making him immeasurably more powerful, but also made any former bullies scared for their lives where they'd previously lorded over his. He wore size ten shoes and packed on a couple of stones of muscle before many of his bullies' voices had fully broken.

Unfortunately for them, Darren was not yet the type to forgive and forget the cowardly punches thrown and the constant, vicious, relentless racism hurled at the small black kid in class. Those assaults were seared into his brain. The bullies had taunted him, made him feel scared to go to school and driven his confidence through the floor. One by one, each bully got their just desserts from a now toweringly powerful, explosive athlete with the body of an adult but harbouring the memories of that small scared youth, afraid of where the next bout of bullying would come from. Social justice came full circle. Those bullies never bullied again.

Darren changed his name to Campbell to honour his mother's side of the family, not only because his father's side were unknown to him, but also to espouse his mother's values and ensure he would not fall into a life on the street. Track and field athletics became his saviour. He had experienced personal torment through loss of life already and there was no need for his name to add to the statistics.

Upon joining Sale Harriers, Darren was ahead of the curve, always training with age groups two or three steps ahead of his own. This would not only force him to improve rapidly to keep up. It also exposed him to the more mature mannerisms and comportment of those older than him. Mum Marva's moral stance and his academically excellent sister Sophia gave Darren some strong role models at home and now, Darren's social circle encompassed people with a different view on life to the gang members on the streets in Sale Racecourse and Moss Side. Darren's horizons were broadening as track and field athletics forced him to become aware and more attuned to people from different socioeconomic circumstances.

He was also becoming known for being good at running. This brought Darren a level of good notoriety, a concept foreign to him having enjoyed the bad kind at school for so long. Dave Law's intervention had taught Darren the value of concentration and focus and these aspects were being magnified at Sale Harriers by coaches equating hard work on the track with success. Darren's problem with authority figures was becoming less of an issue the more he understood they were setting a path from which he could learn and benefit. He started to appreciate that whether it was a teacher instructing in school or a coach instructing at the track, this wasn't necessarily instruction and control for its own sake. He could take something beneficial from it.

Nevertheless, the gravitational pull of the streets was a strong one. Those closest to him were also under the influence of the factors that made social progression a glass ceiling for many from their neighbourhood. The temptation to make an easy buck through illegality was a constant backdrop and many shrugged their shoulders to the immorality. It was just what people did.

Darren was part of a gang that came very close to robbing a pub – not in some daring heist in order to raise funds - but rather as an act of living up to a stereotype of being in a gang. They didn't ultimately go through with it because on the way to the watering hole in question, Darren's bike suffered a flat tyre which took the wind out of the whole escapade. There was also a hair-raising incident at the Royal Exchange Shopping Centre in Manchester where five rival gang members took a dislike to a person that Darren merely happened to be out shopping with that day. A fight ensued and Darren was lunged at with a knife. The knife tore through the long leather jacket he was wearing that day passing within inches of his midriff, the swaying contours of the coat momentarily concealing the position of his body within and saving Darren from possible fatal injury.

Things were brought to a head when 'T' (one of those friends forever known by his nickname) got involved with people even more dangerous than those they knew around Sale Racecourse. This act of venturing outside of his neighbourhood and safe zone resulted in T being shot and killed. Darren and his friends had become inured to the shootings, murders, robberies all around them but this was the first instance that had affected them personally. The pain was indescribable. Seeing their mothers and brothers cry uncontrollably while attempting to maintain their fragile, misguided idea of dignity was heart-breaking for the boys. They realised that it wasn't just one life that was affected when they came face to face with the family's agony and that they needed to change course. The murder remained unsolved, just another statistic to reinforce the image of 'Gunchester.' Darren had to distance himself from his roots or they would grow and suffocate him. He needed his own space to carve out a future away from distractions, away from his past and in the company of those that shared similar dreams.

THE SALE HARRIER BECAME EUROPEAN JUNIOR CHAMPION IN 1991 and World Junior silver medallist in both sprint events in Seoul a year later, behind a certain Trinidadian named Ato Bolton. A year running on the Golden League circuit in Europe the following season seemed a sure springboard to greater things but injury, disillusionment and an awareness of the dark side of sport put paid to the dream very swiftly. Within a year of being told that one of the best ways to heal from an injury was to take drugs ("everyone else is doing it"), Campbell was trialling for Millwall reserves against Arsenal and scoring goals for Weymouth FC. And yet the self-awareness that had ensured his ability to survive on the roughest streets for so long allowed him an understanding that he had been blessed as an athlete.

Enter Linford Christie, Colin Jackson, Katherine Merry, Math Elias, Jamie Baulch et al. Darren joined what was an elite sprinting club of around ten athletes whose names adorned the highest rankings of world athletics during the mid-nineties. Within months of returning to the track he was on the way to the Atlanta Olympics where his face would be plastered over the newspaper sports pages. He became the chosen poster boy of a team that had failed to get the baton around in the men's sprint relay. A year later, a bronze at the Athens World Championships prefaced a gold in the 100m at the European Championships at Budapest. The rollercoaster will-he-or-won't-he highs and lows of Darren Campbell's track career were so precipitous, you could imagine that every year in the teachers' staff room at Ashton-on-Mersey, a different member of staff could be sipping their coffee over lunch and telling another, "I told you so."

Dave Law was proven right at about 9:32am London time on September 28th 2000 when his former pupil was leading the field in the final of the Olympic men's 200m at the Sydney Olympic stadium with nothing or nobody between him and the finish line except the darkening Australian skies. He was around forty metres from becoming an Olympic champion when Konstantinos Kenteris's injection of vitality and pace took him from fourth to first in the blink of an eye. Campbell's silver was a phenomenal achievement, but this silver lining was in need of a cloud. This duly came the following day when the relay team crashed out of the heat in farcical circumstances, Campbell watching from the sidelines in despair.

This Olympic springboard launched Campbell not to further successes, but headlong into a two-year period of injury, depression and introspection, involving personal heartache and the soul-destroying feeling - which he had experienced as a son - of being an absent father on Christmas Day. The highs and lows kept coming for Campbell, with 2001 being a career write off before he fought tooth and nail to be remotely ready to appear at the 2002 Commonwealth Games. He relied on grit, passion and aggression to fight for a bronze and a gold in front of his home crowd, achieving an unlikely victory and fittingly bringing his career full circle to where it started in Manchester.

The Darren Campbell career rollercoaster was never a smooth ride. Like Moss Side in the 1980s, something was always going to blindside you.

HOW THE LAYMAN THINKS ABOUT SPRINTERS AND THEIR TRAINING regime goes something like this. Powerful, laidback, black, alpha-males and females, naturally gifted and explosive, that do a quick rep on the track in the sun before taking twenty minutes rest until the next time. The absence of words such as "resilient", "dedicated" and "relentless" speak volumes on how they are perceived. Usain St Leo Bolt from Jamaica was an athlete for nigh-on eleven years before becoming an overnight success. His coach Glen Mills nurtured a tall, scoliosis-suffering sprinter over the course of many years into being an efficient superstar, able to cope with the demands of running quicker than any human being in history across three events in an Olympic Games. Yet what do people think of when they think about Bolt, apart from running 9.58 seconds for the 100m? Chicken Nuggets. Late nights partying. Doing whatever he wanted to do and still turning up to make the rest of the world's best sprinters look frozen in time.

Even though Bolt spent countless hours running on slow grassy tracks, towing rusty weights behind him for innumerable repetitions, his 'greatness' and 'talent' rendered all of that moot. His genetic ability became the sole reason for his success, ignoring any chance that his work ethic might have been phenomenal behind the smokescreen of late nights, that his dedication might have been at such a high level that he could afford to indulge sporadically in takeaway chicken nuggets and that his coaching regime under Mills and others could be more sophisticated and appropriate for his talents than all the other competing biomechanists, knowledge-leaders and coaching pioneers world wide would privately admit, even to themselves. It would be uncomfortable in the extreme to the sporting status quo that an old Jamaican coaching with rusty gear on a grass track could be more attuned to the needs of a small-margin event such as sprinting than high performance directors of governing bodies in richer nations.

While Bolt was carving out his career and showing the world what 'elite performance' truly was, Allyson Felix was doing the same in female sprinting, becoming the most successful track and field athlete in history. Both Bolt and Felix, through coaches Mills and in Felix's case Bob Kersee, husband of legendary Olympic Champion Jackie Joyner-Kersee, had been placing extensive emphasis on over-distance work, strength and speed maintenance in their training. Bolt's success when broken down in an event-demand sense, showed that he was the quickest man over 100m ever, not just due to his raw speed, but for his amazing ability to maintain upwards of 26mph for an amount of time unusual even amongst the other superhumans of track and field. The taxing sessions that honed and forged this ability were a result of widening the gaze from what conventional training looked like for sprinting. From a coaching perspective, both Bolt and Felix adopted methods that were not the kind of work usually associated with their discipline.

This narrative of what constituted speed training was encouraged by a scientific approach that went down a research rabbit hole of muscle fibre-types, genetic lineage and even biomechanical gait analysis. This approach gained ground, almost away from sport altogether, lending credence to the idea that sprinting success was genetically predetermined. If this was the case, traditional training paradigms were fine. The fastest person would just win, as long as nothing went awry on the day. Instead of widening the gaze a little on the thousand variants that lead to Olympic sprint success, a common narrative in sport, society, even academia led to a doubling-down on the notion of genetic predetermination.

The gene in question, which was said to lead to advantageous muscle fibre types, the actn3- a molecular protein - was found to be 5% more prevalent in the Jamaican genetic lineage than in other nations' when it came to elite sprinters. But what does this argument lead us to think about the predictive power of genes when it comes to success? An excellent research study in 2015 highlighted what its authors Hughey and Goss described as being a 'reinforced racial essentialism' when it came to building stereotypes around black athletes' portrayal in the media when discussing sporting success.

> "Recent mainstream journalism has collectively advanced the proposition that black athletic success is the product of little more than genetic traits."[1]
>
> — Hughey & Goss

This study dissected almost three hundred newspaper, media and research articles between 2003 and 2014, and found a bias within the media to construct a narrative of black athletes' success to be down to biology, with whites athletes' successes down to hard work and intelligence. A brawn vs brain narrative was found to exist even as late as 2014.

What about socioeconomic factors such as Darren's ability to see athletics as a means of breaking out of a cycle of gang life in Manchester? Cultural factors such as Jason's ability to view sporting success as a means of acceptance and equality in a society in Bath that had up to that point, given him none? What about the personal effect of Mark being introduced and inspired by his father to take up athletics, or the fickleness and fortune of Marlon discovering a love and a talent for the sport at a comparatively late age? Without these intervening factors, it's unlikely that any of these guys would have discovered and then mastered sprinting, no matter how fast their genes said they were.

TV programmes and articles contained a narrative that there might have been an element of survival of the fittest through slavery, some genetic sifting which resulted in a superior sporting gene becoming dominant, but serious research labels this notion preposterous. Even if this were possible, it would take over fifty generations to manifest. Around 1500 years at least. This narrative reaching and grasping was a doubling down on a weak and lazy hypothesis: that black athletes had a biological advantage by virtue of racism-inspired and slavery-induced accelerated Darwinism. By definition, this hypothesis suggested that these athletes were genetic beneficiaries of the tragedies and torture of their forebears and therefore were fast because of luck.

Bizarrely, team sport athletes began to find themselves being measured and judged on distance covered in games, bouts of effective work completed and other capacity-based attributes rather than actual contributions to the game they were playing. In the search for an edge, sport began to look elsewhere for answers and while some previously ignored routes to optimisation may have been uncovered, there was a general danger of over-indexing on the wrong thing.

While sprinting was being explained by how genetically suited the person was to the event, the performance capabilities of endurance athletes were being categorised through lung capacity, red blood cell count and increased training volumes, their numbers eulogised by sports media. By contrast, sprinters looked like the lazy cousins. Bolt had to be 'the most talented athlete ever' and 'a freak of nature' to achieve his rarefied level of success, an impression not helped by athletes falling foul of doping regulations while trying to best him, thereby making his efforts feel suspicious.

This stereotype followed British athletes during their careers and was especially ironic in the case of Darren Campbell. Here was an athlete who had come through hardships and personal pain unbeknownst to the majority of sportspeople, all before he had ever even stepped on to a track.

Darren's upbringing, his experiences on the street, the lack of a father figure and the fleeting nature of any financial security had all played their part in creating a steely person with an ability to recognise and cope with life's bumps. What he hadn't seen coming was the frequency and height of those bumps once he had left Manchester. Existing in the cutthroat world of professional sport - especially in an event where the top three could make enormous amounts of money and the rest barely make a living – brought heavy stresses. He had many plates spinning at any one time and in the attempt to keep them all from crashing, he found that he was in fact the one most likely to fragment into a thousand pieces.

The 2002 Manchester Commonwealth Games had taken an emotional toll. Darren felt that he owed a debt of gratitude to many back in his home city. In managing to discover the ability to outperform his presumed physical capacities at that time to win two medals, he felt at peace. Many people from his past were heavily emotionally invested in his success and he had always wanted to pay tribute to those that had taken care of him during his time on the Sale Racecourse streets. By putting on a show, he'd paid that debt with interest and could focus on moving forward.

The prospect of training and developing now filled him with gusto. Campbell recommitted himself to his craft in earnest, embracing new ideas and pushing his body to new limits of strength and power. A return to family life had also given him back his zestful persona and filled him with energy and for the first time in his career, everything was pointing in the same direction at the same time. He felt settled at home and in training where a new confidence based on his recent accomplishments provided the bedrock for an assault on track and field. Darren won the 100m at the British Championships which also acted as the World Championship trials at the Alexander Stadium, Birmingham, finishing ahead of Mark Lewis-Francis and Jason Gardener. Jason and Darren's story intertwined further during this period, Darren had by this time linked up with Jason's former coach Dave Lease and Jason with Darren's former coach Malcolm Arnold.

One of the aspects Darren had been working on forensically was his start. He had employed scientific expertise through working with force platforms and immediate power feedback apparatus at Cardiff Metropolitan University. These devices measured the speed and power of the force applied into the floor upon starting from blocks and Darren learned how to apply pressure quicker, in order to get away quicker. He had significantly improved his power to weight ratio in the gym and was also using a nifty little machine called a start simulator each night before going to bed, a machine that emitted random beeps to simulate the marks-set-go sequence. He was finely tuning his entire life to get away from the blocks quicker than ever before.

What was more important than all this rediscovered dedication to learn and develop was the psychological safety he felt now at home. He, Clair and their son Aaryn were living in South Wales, back together as a fully functioning and happy family unit which gave him a strength far beyond any that could be attained in the gym. Darren was psychologically primed to perform and his body was as ready as his brain. He was comfortable, confident and conditioned, with all three aligning concurrently for probably the first time ever in his career.

The 2003 World Championships signified the end of what history would judge as a pre-Usain Bolt cycle, with success spread amongst several sprinters rather than being seized by one man. Ato Boldon, Maurice Greene, Asafa Powell, Tim Montgomery and Jon Drummond were chasing gold alongside the British contingent of Darren, Dwain Chambers and Mark Lewis-Francis. The field for the men's 100m was as strong and as open as any in recent times. This strength in depth could be viewed in one of two ways. In the absence of one dominant presence who would reduce the rest of the competitors to fighting for the lesser medals, the chance for gold for everyone was elevated. The problem was that while anyone could win it, you had to get there first. The sheer quality of the field and number of potential winners actually reduced an athlete's hope of qualifying for the final in the first place, which is precisely what happened to Maurice Greene, Asafa Powell and Mark Lewis-Francis. The stacked men's 100m field had been whittled down to eight finalists, of which the majority of commentators favoured one of the Americans in Bernard Williams or Tim Montgomery.

The Stade de France was the setting for the championships and former footballer Darren lined up his blocks in lane 7, almost at the exact spot from where Youri Djorkaeff delivered the corner for Zinedine Zidane's second goal in the 1998 football World Cup Final. In lane 6 next to Darren was Tim Montgomery, the world record holder who had set his world record mark of 9.78 seconds at that very stadium a year previously.

The start is always vitally important but in such a close field, it could be decisive. The starter himself had a surprise up his sleeve for the athletes. The Frenchman dictated that the hold between the set position and the gun was *trés petite*, barely a quarter of a second in length. The time Campbell had invested in mastering his own reactions to the gun, from the electronic beeping device at night to the power diagnostics, was all rendered instantly obsolete. The field leapt in unison, almost shocked out of its collective blocks, tearing down the track. Both Campbell and Chambers, with his brawny physical presence dominating his lane, figured well in the start but as the race got to halfway, the presence of Manchester Commonwealth Games champion Kim Collins became evident. Collins was out of the hustle and bustle in lane one, scampering side to side with his staccato, mechanical, stiff running style. The athlete in lane one usually had a very specific role in any 100m race which was to finish between sixth and eighth. That was almost a given. Nobody in lane one ever won anything in the sprints.

Yet away from the maddening crowd of athletes together closing in on the finish line, Collins with his knee-high socks was running his own race. Both Darren and Dwain Chambers strode powerfully in the closing metres to claim medals and as the athletes crossed the line, a heavy collective gasp of astonishment filled the Parisian sky. They had finished in as uniformly a straight line as they had started. The naked eye could barely distinguish between first and last. It seemed that Collins had become World Champion yet at a second glance, could it be Darren Campbell? One could look at the photo-finish image and pick a different winner with each viewing. Even with the benefit of a static photograph, Kim Collins looked the victor but Campbell on the nearside was close enough to create significant doubt. Darrel Brown was squeezed in between them to create further uncertainty.

The result was posted on the screen. Collins had won but the next three athletes were all within a hundredth of a second to themselves being crowned world champion. It was agonising. Despite initially looking that he may have won the whole thing, Darren was awarded bronze behind Darrel Brown.

He had already achieved European and Commonwealth titles prior to Sydney, but since those Olympic games merely thirty months earlier, there had been personal heartache, injury, family trouble, disillusionment with the sport and failure. Yet despite his troubled times, Darren had now come within a hair's breadth of being Olympic 200m champion and World 100m Champion, while also claiming two Commonwealth medals. His success had not been built on any steady climb or linear progression and he'd had to make sacrifices, from being close to his family and friends, financial stability and even his emotional health. It seemed that attaining success for Darren Campbell would always be a fight.

Or perhaps it was that Darren Campbell needed a fight to achieve success?

11

51 WEEKS TO GO
PARIS WORLD ATHLETICS CHAMPIONSHIPS 2003

It was the last week of August and the best athletes from around the world were in Paris taking in the Eiffel Tower, the Arc de Triomphe, and the Jardin des Tuileries. Jason Gardener was not one of them. By finishing third at the British trials, he should by rights have been selected as an individual competitor or as a part of the relay team. He was neither. He had quit the latter disgruntled and disillusioned at its processes and management and was not selected for the former, with Dwain Chambers preferred ahead of him. The *jardins* of Paris would have to wait for Gardener.

Everyone else in Paris was waiting for Jon Drummond. The flamboyant and talented American had false-started in his 100m quarter final and according to the new rules designed to nullify constant gun-jumping, was immediately disqualified. Despite the clarity of the rules and for reasons known to him alone, he didn't see eye-to-eye with the officials. He protested by refusing to move for an hour, holding up all following heats and events in the process. He lay down on the track unwilling to move a muscle, in an attempt either to curry sympathy or to reverse the decision, neither of which was ever going to come. Mark Lewis-Francis and Darren Campbell were both in the next heat and had to wait for over an hour until Drummond's toys were back in the pram and his spikes well and truly off the track. This was not the best way to prepare for a high-level sprint event.

Mark Lewis-Francis's appetite for training was greater than ever. Recent disappointments had fuelled his competitive nature and he felt that physically and psychologically he was in shape to make amends for the disappointment of the Commonwealth Games the previous season. He was still a very young sprinter carving his path in senior athletics but while others his age would be focussed on gathering experience and developing, there was expectation on Mark to perform right now.

Once an athlete began to post quick times or qualified for the British team, there was an expectation to challenge for medals, irrespective of age or competitive experience. Mark had flirted with the ten-second barrier in a meet at Ostrava in the Czech Republic early in the season, proving that his injured hamstring from the previous season could hold up to the stresses of high-level competition. Hard work in the off-season had bulletproofed his muscular conditioning a little more to the rigours of competitive athletic life. Despite his very respectable performances, he was still developing physically and each off-season that went by would strengthen him a little more.

Mark was keen to make an impression as a senior athlete but recognised his position within the informal apprentice system that existed in track and field where younger athletes were expected to sit back and wait their turn. He knew he merited his place at the world championships in both the individual event and the relay but he had little faith that the selection decision would go his way when it came to the latter. This was a matter of concern, for in light of the two golds won the previous summer, the relay team was on a high and ready to challenge the Americans. Missing out on the team almost certainly meant missing out on a medal.

---

18 MONTHS TO GO

FIVE MONTHS EARLIER, AWAY FROM THE BALMY LATE SUMMER Parisian nights, the World Indoor Athletics Championships were held at the significantly less romantic but no less impressive National Indoor Arena in Birmingham, England. Marlon Devonish's training had been progressing beautifully and the Worlds would be held up the road from his home City of Coventry. He had crisscrossed the globe to establish himself as an athlete and now he had the chance to become a World Champion merely a few miles from his family home.

> "I had to go to that, didn't I? The World Champs on my doorstep, just up the road from where I had stepped onto my first ever athletics track at Coventry."
>
> — MARLON DEVONISH

Indoor events had never been a part of Marlon's life, tending to view them as a disruption of his winter training. The occasional appearance would merely serve as a litmus test of how well his winter training was progressing but when he demolished a personal best at a Euro Series event in Birmingham by running a 20.5 second 200m, it prompted a conversation with his coach Tony Lester. The performance at the Euro Series – which had indicated that he was in the shape to run a sub-20 seconds 200m outdoors – was reason enough for Marlon to forgo the Worlds in order to continue on what was evidently a very effective winter programme but Tony Lester interjected. He knew that in athletics that you had to take your opportunities when they came and that Marlon was clearly in the shape to be World Champion. Marlon took Tony's point and once his mind was made up, he went for it wholeheartedly.

It was a surreal and emotional experience for Marlon to make the short journey past his childhood track at Kirby Corner and up the A45 to Birmingham to compete in a World Championships. From where it all began to the top of the world in one day.

He was in tremendous shape, comfortably qualifying for the final of the 200m running with ease and even with joy. Drawn in lane 6 for the final, he knew he would be the target for all the other runners in the one lap indoor dash, all looking at the local boy with glee as a target to chase and a famous scalp to take. He had to keep concentrating as he strode on the hollow floorboards of the indoor track right next to the outer barriers. The ground contact forces involved in running on indoor tracks differ significantly from their outdoor equivalents with each stride's force dissipating with an echo into the raised floor instead of propelling the athlete forward. Due to the surface and the tighter curvature of the track, indoor sprinters need to apportion a small percentage of their concentration to running straight as much as running quickly. Out in lane 6 with his arms and torso close to the advertising hoardings on his right hand side, Marlon had plenty to think about before even considering any rivals.

Thankfully, the next time he saw his competitors was after the finishing line in the post-race congratulatory embraces. He ran from the front and won from the front, becoming world indoor champion a few miles from his childhood home. This victory made people sit up and notice on the world stage, signalling that he belonged at the top level. He'd always felt that he could belong in this company but now his performances validated his ambitions and he returned to his training group in London full of confidence, with the motivation to convert his champion indoor form to an outdoor season.

> "The difference between passion and obsession, is passion knows when to stop!"
>
> — Marlon Devonish

If anything, Marlon Devonish the World Champion was too motivated. Having a taste of success only made him hungry for more and he threw himself into training, adding muscle bulk and pushing himself harder and harder until the fate he was tempting duly delivered. He got injured once again, cranking a handbrake on his hard-earned momentum. This turned his outdoor season into a return to fitness rather than a chance to compete for medals. Nevertheless, the incremental improvements in his performances ensured that he performed well enough in the trials to be selected for the relay at the Paris World Championships.

Marlon had developed a reputation in athletics for versatility and consistency. The problem with being versatile was that everyone saw Marlon as a Swiss Army knife, able to slot into any lineup in any role, so competition workload was always going to be high. By only qualifying for the relay, he would be the freshest squad member and should be able to handle a higher volume of heat and practices. The physical and psychological load of running individual events and relays wears athletes down and the whole competition is often an exercise in preserving energy for the final. Having Marlon solely for the relay ensured a fresher pair of legs, but he found himself filling in for more legs of more relay practices. Relay sessions had become more frequent, an encouraging sign that steps were being taken to improve performances, but in this instance, he found himself shouldering a large workload. The selection for the team itself was somewhat clouded and unclear with Mark Lewis-Francis overlooked for the latter rounds despite featuring in the heats and being at the Championships themselves as an individual semi-finalist in the 100m.

The team had seen Darren reach the final of the 100m and the 200m, medaling in the shorter event and finishing within a whisker of becoming World Champion. Darren's mindset was always one of a big event runner. If his name was on the start list of any final, he would manage to eke out a performance from somewhere, somehow. If Marlon was the resilient one in the team, Darren was the tenacious one. He was always able to emotionally switch on in finals, and this was proven to be the case again in Paris.

> "This time, we all thought the Americans were not only aware of us as a threat, but also worried about us for maybe the first time."
>
> — Darren Campbell

At the Seville 1999 World Championships, the British team had almost beaten the USA. It was a surprise to the watching world but significantly, it made the American team regard the Brits as a serious threat. They knew their crown had slipped slightly but the British calamities in Sydney and Edmonton the following years restored their typical confidence, the status quo restored. It seemed that the British threat had been a flash in the pan.

2003 was different. It was the first time the USA team were less than upbeat about their prospects and they acknowledged a British threat before the event, even acting humble. There was little banter and no trash-talking. Darren Campbell had won a fantastic bronze in the 100m final and finished fourth in the 200m final. The relay team had two 100m finalists in Campbell and Chambers and a world indoor champion in Devonish. As the British team of Christian Malcolm, Darren Campbell, Marlon Devonish and Dwain Chambers entered the call room in the belly of the stadium it was apparent by their mannerisms and nervous glances that the USA saw them as a major threat for the very first time. Britain lined up in lane 5 in the final, with the USA a lane outside in 6. The rivals would be toe to toe from the gun.

While the GB relay team looked like a good prospect for a medal, there was an air of foreboding around the wider British team. They had only three medals to show for their endeavours – a silver for Kelly Holmes in the women's 800m and bronzes for Campbell in the 100m and Hayley Tullett of Swansea Harriers in the women's 1500m. The British press were ready to stick the knife into the underperforming GB Team while the administrators were fearing for the future of the whole endeavour, given that their funding for the next cycle relied in part on their medal tally.

In this men's 4 x 100m relay final, Christian Malcolm was up against the newly crowned 200m World Champion John Capel on the first leg. As the gun went both tore around the first bend and were a yard ahead of the other teams at the first changeover. Malcolm had given Britain a significant boost by staying close to his American adversary as Capel was not only a major weapon for the American team but had been in fine form. The changeover with Darren Campbell was smooth and the stagger with the Americans maintained over the ensuing 100m before Marlon Devonish sprinted away from his mark in anticipation for the handover of the baton. Then as Campbell's sprint reached its conclusion and the opening few strides of Devonish's leg began in earnest, the gap disappeared completely.

Had the Americans fumbled? No they hadn't. Had they run out of their zone? They hadn't erred there either. Even so, the six-foot gap of the stagger had vanished into thin air. The reason was simple, and telling. The baton changeover between Campbell and Devonish was so smooth that they breezed past the Americans effortlessly with Marlon gaining on the lead with each stride of the third leg. Upon realising that the Brits were flowing past on the inside lane, Darvis Patton immediately tightened up and started fighting. His shoulders rocked from side to side where previously they had been relaxed and fluid, only exacerbating the problem. The British team were putting the Americans under pressure for the first time in years and the USA couldn't muster a response. For an American team to hand the baton to their final leg runner and not be in first place was unheard of. The British team had been smooth and composed, simply putting pressure on their rivals to see if they could cope. The answer was a resounding no.

As Devonish closed in on the home straight, the British team were two yards or more ahead of the Americans as Dwain Chambers received the baton. Chambers, barrel-chested and brawny, bolted away down the home straight holding off the somewhat unexpected challenge of Cláudio Roberto Souza from the Brazilian team in lane 4. Chambers and Souza held a consistent gap, with JJ Johnson the American striding knees-high in third unable to make an impression. It looked like an arm-wrestle between Brazil and Britain for the best part of six seconds until both leading teams suddenly seemed to haemorrhage energy and speed with the finish line closing. With around thirty metres to go JJ Johnson, now running the leg of his life, was closing on the Brits quicker than they were closing on the finish line. He reeled in both rival teams and seemed to be gaining speed as he crossed the line, Chambers's dip not enough to grab gold for Britain. Johnson had gotten there first.

Even having lost a seemingly certain gold, the British team were over the moon with their silver once the disappointment had subsided. They felt they deserved it after several barren years and the slow progress from the previous season had sped up, culminating in them scaring the life out of the Americans. They knew that they should have beaten them, but a World silver medal was a decent reward for an ever-improving team of sprinters.

> "I was pissed off at not being chosen to run, of course I was, because I felt that I had deserved my place, but when they got the silver almost winning gold, it was pretty tough to argue with that. I was delighted for the team, of which I was a part of at the end of the day."
>
> — Mark Lewis Francis

Mark Lewis-Francis had been withdrawn from the final team but having featured in the heats, he at least had a silver medal to temper his disappointment. As the only athlete in the squad to feature in the heats but not in the final, he showed the grace and selflessness that was crucial in forming a team for any future championships. Being self-critical as he was, Mark felt that even after gaining a World medal, his athletics career was treading water. At only twenty years old, he was still of the age where he would be deemed to be a future prospect in most sports but by being an early achiever, he was already starting to be labelled as the kid that never achieved his full potential. This weighed heavily on his mind.

Many of the top British sprinters were now being recognised on the world stage for the very first time. The relay silver medal also validated the investment into the British Athletics team, a message that was always pressed hard at each point of failure. They partied hard into the night, enjoying each other's company as friends and teammates instead of as rivals for once. Drink-inspired promises were made where they solemnly promised one another to go one better and win Olympic gold the following season in Athens. A band of brothers was being born out of a history of an underperforming collection of individuals.

JASON GARDENER HAD TRAINED FOR YEARS WITH A CREW OF ELITE pole vault athletes that included Tim Thomas and former Commonwealth gymnast silver medallist Sonia Lawrence. The elements of gymnastics, plyometric and core training involved with this type of training had made him exceptionally strong functionally, improved his flexibility and ultimately made him more durable. It was the winter of 2003 and these aspects were to be tested to their limits by new coach Malcolm Arnold whose conditioning programmes were gruelling and huge on volume. All of Jason's athletic qualities were being scrutinised under the stress of extreme endurance.

After one session, Malcolm Arnold canvassed Jason's opinion about getting him back into the relay team. The silver medal at the Paris World Championships demonstrated that the team had got their act together and Jason was good enough to break his way back into the fold. His was a self-imposed absence and Arnold smoothing the waters, perhaps he could rejoin his compatriots. Gardener's grievances with the slipshod relay team culture had prompted his scathing letter to David Moorcroft but the reports coming back now were of a better level of behaviour, an improved attitude and an intolerance to mediocrity which Gardener had longed for. Much of this improvement was down to the athletes themselves, fed up with being hung out to dry for mistakes that had their roots in a culture of compromise and taking the bull by the horns as a group.

Jason wanted in and a meeting was arranged between Malcolm Arnold and British relay coach Steve Perks. They were close acquaintances from previous coaching experiences and the meeting was constructive, up until Perks suggested that Gardener, in order to pay penance for leaving the squad previously, needed to "go and speak with the boys" to see if they would accept him back into the team.

Arnold's demeanour changed on the spot. He could not believe that this was a serious suggestion. Was this an indictment on a weak system or a window into a setup where the runners ran the show? UK Athletics's stance was that Jason had quit and would need to demonstrate an elevated level of commitment towards the other athletes in order to return. They didn't want to set a precedent of athletes retiring and returning whenever they felt like it. Jason had quit because of UK Athletics not holding themselves to the same professional standards as they demanded of the athletes. There was an impasse. From a performance point of view the Munich relay team had done very well and perhaps UK Athletics felt that they had enough strength in depth in the relay team to glide through to the Olympics the next year. This was soon to change.

MONACO WAS A BEAUTIFUL PLACE FOR THE WORLD'S BEST athletes to prepare for the World Championships. A warm breeze drifted in from the Mediterranean sea across the Stade Louis II stadium which sat immediately adjacent to the beautiful Port de Fontvieille, with superyachts and Ferraris only adding to the air of glamour. Many go to Monaco for its discretion as much as its beauty but privacy was impossible for the athletes, with only one track on a small corner of the French Riviera available to train on. Anyone who was anyone in elite athletics was there.

Darren Campbell remembers the scene well, soaking up the sun while getting in his reps.

After one session, he got chatting to his friend and rival Ato Boldon, being joined in time by the American sprint legend Maurice Greene. The sport of athletics was a cosy business where everyone knew, trained with or occasionally got married to other athletes. It was difficult to keep secrets throughout the season when they were scattered around the globe, let alone when they were all stretching in the same patch of southern European sun.

One secret was on everyone's lips at around this time that, if true, would shake the foundations of world athletics to its core. Strong speculation emanated from America about what was to become known as the BALCO scandal involving athletes coached by Trevor Graham and Remi Korchemny. The sprinting community were hearing whispers about which athletes might be tainted by the spectre of drug-taking. Names were being bandied around, among them some of the biggest in athletics.

Fast forward a few weeks to the Paris World Championships and Mark Lewis-Francis was nursing his disappointment at not being included in the sprint relay team with Dwain Chambers selected in front of him. Darren had the swirling rumours of Monaco fresh in his mind and decided to speak with Mark. The as yet unproven accusations implicated one of the foremost training groups, a group that included Dwain Chambers of Great Britain. Keeping the possibility of a scandal emerging from the championships in mind and in an attempt to soothe Mark's temper, Darren asked him what his preference would be – to win gold here in Paris or be a part of the relay team that would go for gold at the Athens Olympics the next year? Darren hypothesised that if the gossip surrounding Chambers's training group proved to be true, the battle for the final anchor leg spot at Athens would be wide open and that Mark could be crucial to the Team GB effort.

A few days later Britain when snatched defeat from the jaws of victory in the closing strides of the men's 4x100m, there was no frustration etched on Dwain Chambers's face as he was overtaken on the line. Chambers's wry smile in defeat at the end suggested someone who had been running with the weight of the world on his shoulders.

The world was about to find out that indeed, he had been.

> "If you succumb to taking drugs, you are by definition admitting to yourself that you are mentally weak. Not only do you not believe that you are good enough, but you don't think that you will achieve your dreams using your own talents and abilities."
>
> — Jason Gardener

Britain was enjoying an Indian summer in 2003. Marlon Devonish was walking off the training track after finishing what had been an exhausting session at the west London stadium. For Marlon it was the start of his winter preparation for an Olympic year and while he felt buoyed by his silver medal from Paris, he was determined to learn his lesson and not overtrain before a major championship. He was training smartly, combining exertion with rest, balancing listening to his body with cajoling it to places it had never been. His training partners, 400m runners Mark Richardson and Mark Hylton, were perfectly complementing his own training, giving him a flavour of endurance without racking up the excess repetitions which could push him over the edge. There was no need for panic training, no need for huge overloading this time. He'd made his mistakes and what was the point if he didn't learn from them? There was to be no repeat of Sydney.

His phone buzzed in his kitbag by the side of the track. It was his agent. Marlon put on his shades, tossed his bag over his shoulder and took the call as he walked back towards the stands on the far side of the track.

"Sit down Marlon – this is not good news"

Everything froze immediately. Mind racing as to what was wrong, he sat down on the track, phone next to his ear and listened.

As a boy, Jason Gardener had been inspired by the Los Angeles Olympics. Four years later the Games were held in the South Korean city of Seoul and Jason was glued to the spectacle. He'd get up and watch first thing, the time difference between Bath and the South Korean metropolis making getting to school on time a challenge and he was utterly transfixed. The Men's 100m final was a battle between Americans Carl Lewis and Calvin Smith, Canadian Ben Johnson, and Britain's Linford Christie.

Jason's neighbours were an elderly couple who had an arrangement with their young neighbour that he'd collect their shopping for them in exchange for the princely sum of

50p. The Men's 100m final fell on a Saturday morning so before a trip to the centre of Bath, Jason joined them in watching Ben Johnson tilt the world on its axis with his bullet start, destroying the field almost before his rivals had left their starting blocks. Seeing the Canadian blast away from a world class field, winning the race from 97 metres out, was an exhilarating spectacle of raw power and made a huge impression on the young Jason. Johnson became the toast of Canada and the world of athletics in running the 100m in a scarcely believable 9.79 seconds, a performance that was more detonation than decoration. He crossed the line with his arm aloft, proclaiming himself the greatest, running faster than anyone ever had. While Jason watched this momentous event unfold on the television back in Bath, the cameras caught Carl Lewis's face as he crossed the line. He had the look of someone who knew they'd been conned.

Two days later, BBC Sport's Desmond Lynam – the face of the Seoul games for the British audience – looked visibly shaken live on television as he announced to the cameras, "I've just been handed a piece of paper here that, if it's right, it'll be the most dramatic story out of these Olympics, or perhaps any others."

To Jason Gardener, this didn't compute. Drugs were for the down and outs on the streets, with their needles and heroin. To see this in sport simply didn't make any sense. That the winner was a cheat shocked Jason deeply and taught him that he couldn't always trust his eyes. Fifteen years later, he would be personally affected by another athlete's duplicity.

Great Britain's 4 x 100m silver medal at the Paris 2003 World Athletics Championships was to be annulled. The rumours were true. Dwain Chambers, Britain's anchor leg runner in that event, had failed a drugs test for the synthetic steroid THG. All performances associated with him during the period which he either admitted to or was proven to be cheating were consigned to the dustbin of history. Despite the race being possibly one of the best efforts by a British relay team prior to handing over to Chambers on the last leg, his being ironically the clunkiest leg of the four, it was as if it had never happened. The performance was airbrushed from history, the clearest indicator of the team's progress no longer evidence of anything. Chambers's deception didn't merely affect his own career. It cast a shadow over the careers of others.

The medals and performances were rescinded but something else had been lost. There had been a wry smile shared at the end of the race between the British athletes that despite their loss, there was a feeling that the Athens Olympics eleven months later was to be their time where the team would finally mature. That feeling had evaporated completely. The success celebrated on and off the track that night; the laughing, the joking, the embraces were all suddenly completely meaningless, replaced by an atmosphere of suspicion and distrust because of one man's indiscretions. For Marlon, Mark and Darren especially, who had felt close to realising their potential as parts of a collective, all momentum and confidence had been shattered. They had to start from square one once again. This unravelling of a team dynamic and loss of trust was the greater legacy of Dwain Chambers taking the wrong path. A balloon had burst.

> "Dwain didn't need to do that. He was already a fantastic athlete and he would have achieved much more without needing to go down the road he did. I felt this strange empathy for him as well as anger."
>
> — Marlon Devonish

A feeling of anger and resentment over time turned to one of pity and mercy. Some felt that since he had run close to sub 10 seconds as a junior, Chambers simply needed to be patient. The temptation to follow the easy path which had seduced the likes of Marion Jones and Tim Montgomery had claimed Dwain and many felt sorry for him that he needed to do something as demeaning as take drugs. Not only was it sad but any triumph would ultimately be hollow. An athlete would know that, even if their secret never got out.

Many clean athletes lost money as well as medals in the aftermath of the BALCO scandal. Athletes' contracts with sponsors often contained win bonuses and contract boosts and to get these taken away after the fact because of someone else's transgressions was especially galling. Marlon started counting the money he had lost, visualised the medal he no longer owned and struggled with the emotional loss of a teammate. He thought, "I trusted you." This became a foundation for Marlon with the new relay venture. He needed to know if they were going to do this, that they were truly serious.

For Jason Gardener the BALCO scandal, which included Tim Montgomery, Marion Jones and many others as well as Chambers, highlighted that the same old disease still existed within athletics. The presumption that as time wore on the sport got cleaner with each Olympics being labelled as the "cleanest ever", took a heavy hit to the solar plexus, leaving a bitter taste for Jason. Even still, he believed it created an opportunity for the 2004 Athens games to prove that a team could win in the right way and that by doing so, Britain could salvage some respect.

Having been overlooked for the Paris relay team, Chambers's ban meant something different to Mark Lewis-Francis. It meant that the anchor leg of the relay needed someone to step up and bring the baton home and that Mark had an opportunity to cement his place in the quartet. In 2004 Mark Lewis-Francis had achieved World and European junior medals as well as qualification for an Olympic Games and World Championship, all by the age of twenty. His immediate feeling upon hearing about Dwain Chambers was one of sadness that he had fallen into a trap and that Dwain's name would be forever tarnished. Athletics was a sport that forgave some but made sporting pariahs of others. Seeing the fall of Chambers from world star to outcast made Lewis-Francis even more determined to create as good a name for himself as possible and never tarnish it.

THE BALCO SCANDAL WAS THE CATALYST FOR BRITAIN WINNING gold in Athens. The athletes just didn't know it yet. All the aspects that demonstrated a lack of team-ethic, including politics of selection, lateness for meetings, no-shows for practices, fast-food stops instead of being on time for team-mates, compromising on travel arrangements, injuries, in-house disputes, lack of practice, perceptions of tardiness, failures of leadership – all led up to the Chambers ban. The team was on its knees, with a year to go to the Olympic Games.

Britain now had to qualify for Athens. Their position in the world rankings had plummeted. Whoever the new British four would be were facing rainy days in Crystal Palace and Sheffield working for relay qualification instead of travelling to hot, glamorous locations for camps and competitions. They had to start from scratch. Abandoning this path for the pursuit of personal individual glory must have been entertained by more than a few of the wider group who had a decision to make; come together, lay it all on the line and work as one team to qualify for the Olympics or pack it in. There was nothing to be gained by carrying on half heartedly and the British relay brand was now as toxic as ever.

The relay squad was extremely vulnerable at that moment. There was seemingly nothing to gain and everything to lose to be associated with such a plummeting marque. In a landscape where perception was important, both from a marketing point of view as well as maintaining a competitive sense of superiority, being tagged as a try-hard needing to qualify was the track and field equivalent of playing a midweek, first-round replay against a non-league team in the FA Cup - and not just once. Darren had often highlighted the benefits of competing at the smaller, national league standard meets in order to iron out creases in performance but that was in order to ease into a season. This was entirely different and would require some humility. The athletes needed to show that their egos could be set aside for the greater good. At that point, personality was more important than performance.

In the end, they decided to put their heart and souls into competing as the GB team. They would go to practice and qualify in unheralded and meek surroundings, knowing that the rest of the world would be poking fun at how far they had fallen. Nevertheless, if they stuck together and lived the values that they said were important to them, they believed that anything was possible.

It was unheard of to put as much time into relays as Britain did that year. Jason was back in the team, finding an environment far more switched on than the one he'd left. Firstly, the members were more committed, their willingness to qualify in B-level events testament to this. There was a code of conduct installed and enforced and they were more organised, with clear goals and targets to work towards. These simple processes dovetailed with a clear enforcement of standards from within. Had the management listened to the warnings laid out in his letter?

12

MARK LEWIS-FRANCIS

"We came from shitty backgrounds. Things going wrong was the default setting. Any time something good happened to me, something bad always happened at the same time."

— Mark Lewis-Francis

As Mark Lewis-Francis was walking to the bus stop on his way to another evening training session at Alexander Stadium, Birmingham, a car pulled up alongside him. The window was rolled down and the voice from inside whispered menacingly, "What are you doing around here? We don't like your kind around here."

Miss Francis had only known hard work. She came from Jamaica to live in the United Kingdom and brought with her an impressive work ethic that proved necessary to survive in her new homeland. Arriving in the multicultural area of

Smethwick, she could be forgiven for feeling that they would be universally welcome but as her son Mark was to find out, racism could still rear its ugly head at any moment.

Mark's grandparents from the Lewis side of the family gave him a place to call home for a few years and sport was constantly humming through the house. They especially loved cricket. Their West Indian lineage combined with that part of the world's utter dominance of the sport in the eighties gave them immense pride, something they shared with many expatriate Jamaicans. This era of West Indies cricket was their most successful, with the likes of Malcolm Marshall and Joel Garner justifiably feared as fast bowlers and Sir Vivian Richards and Desmond Haynes living nightmares for the world's fielders with the bat. They were fantastic to watch, full of charisma as well as a fierce competitiveness and their popularity transcended national allegiance. It wasn't all sport at home for Mark as when grandad Lewis didn't have cricket on the television, he had Mark shovelling horse manure in the allotments. This was partly out of necessity but grandad Lewis also wanted to show Mark how working hard could bring tangible reward. Their diligence in the allotment was only outweighed by the sheer amounts of manure carried up and down in rusty wheelbarrows. The hard work paid off; their runner beans, carrots, and pumpkins were always the largest and the best.

One evening around the dinner table, Mark's sister Melissa was whistling an annoyingly catchy tune, the theme song to the BBC's coverage of the Barcelona Olympics by Freddie Mercury and Montserrat Caballé. Soon, ten-year-old Mark and Melissa would be singing this song whenever they weren't glued to the television watching the Olympic spectacle unfold. Linford Christie, a black man from England with West Indian lineage like Mark, won gold in the 100m and an instant connection was made. Music's ability to transport people to a particular time and place worked its magic on Mark, the song conjuring warm memories of family and acting as a reminder of his own ambitions. He would guard this emotional connection for his entire athletics career.

Mark's father had left the UK for Jamaica for work reasons in 1995 when Mark was a teenager. Mark's love for athletics continued to prevail over his friends telling him to stay with them and 'chill', but getting to the track to practice became an ordeal. His mum was working three jobs in order to get food to the table for her children, going to bed very early due to her early starts. The only solution was to take public transport from Grove Lane over to Alexander Stadium at Perry Barr. If Mark wanted to keep the flames of his interest in athletics burning, he'd have to stoke the fire himself. His mother and grandfather had taught him that as a young black man in England, he'd most likely have to jump over a few extra hurdles merely to achieve parity with others, but with the amount of crime on the streets and the poverty around Smethwick, catching three buses at night in an area increasingly blighted by drugs was an unexpectedly high wall to clear. These were the kind of barriers that would never occur to middle class children with two parents, who could be ferried by car to their sporting clubs by a parent that didn't have three jobs. Consequently, Mark learnt self-reliance at a young age.

Training started at 6:30pm. Any latecomers were met with friendly derision from the other athletes at Birchfield Harriers, who took pride in the professional culture instilled throughout the age groups. This dedication and discipline required to merely get to the track on time tested Mark's love for the sport at a very early age. Getting to Alexander Stadium was hard, training itself was hard and yet the hardest part was to come. He usually had to find his own way home, do his homework and find something to eat. If he wanted to continue his quest to become a successful athlete, this regimen had to be followed and he knew that he was on his own. If he was to become successful in athletics, this was the only way. No-one was there to help him. It was either this or give up. This level of sacrifice and dedication was often overlooked by those in later years that questioned his passion and commitment.

For Mark, persistence beat resistance but success would never come easy to him. There was no straight line to glory, for him or for the British team. While an exceptional or exceptionally lucky few might achieve without experiencing hardship, sacrifice and setback, most sporting success doesn't come about without meeting stiff resistance. The British relay team's journey to getting to Athens had already been mired in failure, disappointment and overcoming hurdles. The rocky road has its value in teaching people in all walks of life the vital lesson that when things get uncomfortable, they have to be resilient and resourceful and this team never encountered a smooth, straight road. They had never experienced comfortable. There was always either someone or something in front of them, in a sport where the very definition of success was in nobody finishing in front of you.

Silver medal mentality became a 21st century buzzword. It meant to have the attitude of always believing that there was someone better than you, demanding that you draw on further reserves of effort to win gold. It supplanted the previously-popular mantra of "having a champion attitude" or "believing that you were the best" which could mistakenly foster the belief that an athlete was talented and didn't need to work as hard as others. These terms were approximately twenty-five years behind the events that coined them. One only has to recall the rivalry between Daley Thompson and Jurgen Hingsen where each thought the other was a step ahead, spurring the two on to ever greater heights. Another common concept was that those constantly chosen second or put 'on the bench' often became successful later on in life outside of their sporting careers due to developing the need to analyse, apply and be more industrious than others that were chosen first all the time. In the case of Mark Lewis-Francis, here was a clear example of an athlete needing to go over and above the efforts of others merely in order to train. His mentality wasn't rooted in a competitive drive to get from silver to gold. He needed to be uncommonly motivated to even get to the track in the first place.

Mark's dedication and sacrifice was necessary for him to just participate in track and field athletics. His training partners either drove themselves to the track or were picked up and dropped off by family or friends. Each and every training night, Mark had a ready-made reason to not go to training. Logistics and the sheer effort involved were perpetual barriers for him, barriers absent for all others.

> "It was hard to fit in where I grew up, but when I was at the track, not only did I feel that I was fitting in, but it was world stars like Denise Lewis and Katharine Merry that were the ones going out of their way to make young athletes like me feel appreciated and a part of their crew. I mean, how can you not love that?"
>
> — Mark Lewis-Francis

Training at Alexander Stadium in the 1990s certainly had its benefits. After training, Mark always made a point of having a snack at the stadium café before going home as this was the best part of the night. A fifteen-year-old budding athlete sitting with his coach, devouring a jacket potato with beans and cheese, would see his heroes walk by to grab their snacks before heading home themselves. Over the months and years, young Mark exchanged glances, then chit-chat, then training advice from the likes of Denise Lewis, Katharine Merry and Du'ane Ladejo, athletes that he'd seen on the television with his grandfather. To be able to train next to them, talk to them, for them to be so accessible while embodying what he wanted to achieve was overwhelming. This was magic. To be recognised and appreciated for his efforts by some of the greatest athletes in the world gave him immense confidence that in time, he could emulate them. Following this twice-weekly experience that made him feel like he was walking on air, he had his inevitable three bus rides home in the dark to look forward to. He would sit, resting his sore legs against the steel seats of the bus, each bump giving his limbs a constant reminder of his efforts on the track hours earlier, listening to his headphones and watching the world go by through the Birmingham darkness.

Athletics became the outlet which took Mark away from other distractions that could have led down some very dark paths. His coach Steve Platt played a huge role in keeping him on the straight and narrow. As Mark improved in leaps and bounds, Steve was sacrificing more and more time with his own family in order to help his protégé achieve his goals. This did not go unnoticed by Mark who had learned through his own family the importance of dedication, sacrifice and loyalty. The quicker Mark ran, the more column inches he generated in the athletics papers leading to a degree of notoriety and fame within athletics circles and the usual whispers about the benefits of changing coaches soon followed. Steve Platt had the authorities pressuring him to let Lewis-Francis move to a 'more established' training group elsewhere but Steve trusted Mark and more importantly, Mark trusted Steve. Steve had been committed to him and Mark, whose only real goal was to run a home straight in less than ten seconds, felt committed to Steve.

WHEN ROMANIAN SUPERSTAR NADIA COMĀNECI ACHIEVED THE first perfect score of 10.0 at the 1976 Montreal Olympic Games, the world was equally astonished and aghast at the fact that Comāneci was only fourteen years of age at the time. How could someone so young perform routines to that level of perfection? How many unknown falls, injuries, how much enforced discipline and suffering was behind her performance? Essentially, how far had she been deprived of her childhood in order to achieve a perfect 10?

Comāneci had started training properly as a gymnast in Onesti, Romania at the age of six. Even by the age of fourteen, she had been honing her craft for eight years. During these eight developmental years, the technique, experience and physical and mental demands of the sport had been ingrained within Comāneci. Once her performance levels were deemed worthy to be judged and tested at the highest level, Nadia Comāneci was chosen to perform and win at the Olympics. Two decades later this philosophy had pivoted slightly. Young Manchester United footballer Ryan Giggs, under a new athlete-centred holistic model, was held back from the limelight and very carefully managed. His manager, his significant influences and even some past professionals engineered an environment where he was protected from some of the more nefarious aspects of press intrusion in order to maximise his precocious talent. Both athletes achieved extreme levels of success by taking very different paths.

> "A lot of people do think that you are one of the phenomenal talents that we have had over the last decade or so that has never really produced what you could have done."
>
> — BBC COMMENTATOR JOHN INVERDALE TO MARK LEWIS-FRANCIS, EUROPEAN CHAMPIONSHIPS BARCELONA 2010

Mark Lewis-Francis had pulled up outside Alexander Stadium with his dad in the car and became inquisitive at what the large building was when he was twelve years of age. Just over three years later at the age of 16 he became the World 100m Youth champion in the Polish city of Bydgoszcz. Due to his eye-wateringly quick times as a junior he quickly found himself on the performance treadmill, being selected to run in elite events. There was no graded preparation time for Mark, no long-term athletic development plan, no crossing off competencies and targets as he progressed and matured. He wasn't exposed to years of intense training outside of the limelight like Comaneci or his introduction to senior competition managed with kid gloves like Giggs. Mark wasn't given the luxury of time spent training in the shadows before being thrust in front of the stadium lights. At the age of seventeen, as a raw bright talent, he qualified for the Olympic Games as well as became World Junior Champion. This all happened after only two to three years' worth of training.

How many seventeen year olds qualify for the Olympic Games and choose not to go? The level of maturity shown by Mark and his coach Steve Platt in this respect was astonishing. Sharron Davies was 13 when she attended her first Olympic Games in Montreal and seventeen when winning silver at Moscow. Amir Khan was seventeen when winning his silver medal in Athens. Ade Mafe lined up in the 200m Olympic Final in Los Angeles at the age of seventeen. The temptation for Lewis-Francis must have been overwhelming, especially considering that there was simply no guarantee that he would ever qualify again. Not deciding to go was an act of confidence in his ability as well as acknowledgment of the distance he had to travel to be an Olympic Champion.

Yet there was no celebration. There was no excitement or understanding. He was already being dubbed as an "unfulfilled talent". Respected commentators weighed in, their status giving their pronouncements great credence, that Lewis-Francis was already someone struggling to maximise his ability. Mark was not so much making the leap between junior and senior athletics but precariously bridging both with a foot in each, trying to gain a solid platform from which to progress and gain confidence. Due to his premature elevation up the rankings tables, he had inadvertently deprived himself of the training years in order to learn his craft which benefited the likes of Comāneci, whilst also placing a target on his own back by not being given the same graces as a Giggs in being carefully managed into the bear pit of sport at the highest level. He could not control the latter and the disappointing factor was that many of those undermining his exploits as a raw junior were themselves all too familiar with the pitfalls of making the change into senior sport. When rival athletes were in their late teenage years, learning how to condition and train properly away from the spotlight, Mark was already competing on the senior level.

Young athletes at the time enjoyed nothing more than reading about their exploits in newspapers, especially when they were successful. Mark found that there was a wide disconnect between what he thought were his overachievements and what he was reading in the press, where there was no doubt that what could be a brash and confident public persona counted against him. He was branded as a raw, carefree rogue from a dicey area of Birmingham, someone that needed a dose of personal discipline and maturity lest he become a wasted talent. This created a self-fulfilling prophecy where he not only gained an immediate distrust of those able to comment so eloquently yet erroneously on who he was, but led to a closing in on the walls of trust. He tightened his circle to those that had already gained his trust, people who he knew were on his side. Steve Platt was one of those people.

Steve Platt demanded high standards of his athlete. Despite being thick-set, muscular and strong, Mark never indulged heavily in weight training or plyometrics, bucking a significant trend at the time. Almost all of his training sessions were on the track where he would run endless 150m or 200m repetitions, elevating his fitness levels as well as testing his mental fortitude. This regime reminded Mark of the discipline that his grandfather had instilled in him at the allotment carting horse manure around. Unglamorous, unpleasant, yet beneficial. Not working hard hardly worked. He trusted Steve like he trusted his grandfather and the notions of hard work and trust became cornerstones of what Mark Lewis-Francis stood for and looked for in other people.

Mark was the first in his family to have a lot of things. There was no sounding board within the family on how to cope with various situations so he had to seek out advice from people that were already in the game. His manager Ricky Simms was able to guide him through the business end of athletics and he had full faith in his coach but Mark had to learn to trust his own instincts, the test of which was around the corner. It seemed everything was being thrown at him sooner than he was ready for.

The 2000 Olympic Games trials were held at Mark Lewis-Francis's home track at Alexander Stadium and the seventeen-year-old local boy finished third behind Dwain Chambers and Darren Campbell. He had qualified for the Olympic Games in Sydney at the same venue that had initially ignited his passion for the sport. His was a romantic story. But so was Jason Gardener's. Jason's dream was the same as Mark's but being seven years older, he was effectively two Olympiads worse off in terms of time. Gardener had finished fourth in the race thereby failing to qualify automatically and was practically inconsolable afterwards. As Mark ventured up to the Birchfield bar – the venue for his post-training jacket potatoes with his childhood heroes – he saw the devastated Jason with his coach Dave Lease in the corner. He saw a fellow athlete's dream extinguished and what the pain of that loss looked like first hand. Jason had enjoyed his best year as a senior athlete the previous season but with the tantalising prospect of the Olympic Games looming on the horizon, overapplied his efforts in training. He pushed himself too hard in his personal quest to achieve his dream and minor injuries had affected his preparation. Finishing fourth was fate's cruel sense of humour taunting him.

The rivalry and playful animosity on-track between athletes often turned into respect and admiration off-track. Jason Gardener was an athlete whom Mark respected enormously. Quietly too, Mark and Steve had decided together that should he qualify for the Olympics, they shouldn't view competing at them as a foregone conclusion. While Mark was viewed as an amazing new talent in British sprinting, Steve Platt had given a lot of careful thought to planning Mark's career. He had so much trust and faith in Mark, he believed they should entertain the thought of foregoing the Sydney Olympics to run at the World Junior Championships in Chile instead. He knew Mark's time would come and that he was too young and inexperienced to be thrust into the spotlight and under the microscope of an Olympic Games just yet. Despite being still a junior athlete, the magic had hit home for Mark at those trials because it was the first time he competed against and beat his elder peers. Many of his opponents on the track that day were his boyhood heroes and when he was faced with the prospect of taking such an opportunity away from one of them, the combination of the idea to forego the Olympics and the respect he held for his fellow athlete solidified the decision. The image of a crestfallen Gardener reinforced the idea of how emotionally critical the Olympics were to people and he knew in his heart of hearts that this wasn't the time for him. The decision was made; he was going to Chile. To be able to trust his own judgment and that of his coach to that extent, to forgo the short term in service of a larger vision, was a real act of maturity for a seventeen-year-old.

Showing respect for others was important to Mark. Denying himself a place at the Olympics was ultimately in order to prepare himself better for further battles down the line but his gesture didn't go unnoticed by his fellow athletes, many of whom might not have done the same thing. The respect between Mark and the other British athletes arguably had its genesis in this moment, a respect that would pay dividends in four years' time.

2 YEARS TO GO

A couple of years later, Mark was asked to take part in a publicity shoot for the 2002 Manchester Commonwealth Games. As he pulled up at the venue, a sense of déjà vu hit him similar to the one that occurred with his father outside Alexander Stadium years earlier. He stopped the car outside the City of Manchester Stadium and took a deep breath. The stadium looked absolutely phenomenal. He knew then that the Commonwealth Games were going to be an amazing spectacle in such a theatre, one like he'd never seen firsthand. He drove home to Birmingham a lot more anxious and excited for the event than when he drove up. Psychologically, the Games had already started for him.

The trials to represent England at those Games were held at that same stadium. Construction on what would eventually become the home of the Manchester City football team had only begun a year or so previously, to the extent that the stand was not yet fully built at the start line of the 100m. However, instead of this gaping hole creating the perception of an unfinished building site, it somehow added to the grandeur of the location, like looking into the skeleton of a mythical beast. Mark won the trials, almost running ten seconds exactly and backed up by a strong season in Europe that year, felt confident for the Games.

Running the 100m at the Commonwealths, he took the advice of his coach and held his effort during the qualifying rounds, conserving his energy and ready to unleash all his power in the final. A strong field including fellow Englishmen Jason Gardener and Dwain Chambers as well as soon-to-be world champion Kim Collins, made this sprint medal chase especially competitive but Mark's recent form and performances in the lead up suggested the possibility of a podium finish. Race night was beautiful, still and warm, and as the gun went in a packed City of Manchester Stadium, Mark had a great start. Moving through 30m and 40m, Kim Collins began to assert dominance with his staccato high-speed gait but Mark was on his shoulder moving through the gears. As he went to step on the gas for the final half of the race, a hot, searing, zipping sensation tore from behind his knee up to his backside. A handbrake was pulled at 25mph. Mark's hamstring tore while he was in the middle lane in full flight, about to challenge for gold. He ran through the line, damaging the hamstring with each stride but despite crossing the line, he was no longer part of the race.

He didn't feel frustration or desolation. He felt an acute embarrassment. He could not believe that he'd done this in front of such a large crowd, both in the stadium and watching on their televisions. Of course there was disappointment at not having seized a chance to win a medal, but he felt more mortified and bewildered than angry. He wanted the track to swallow him up.

His embarrassment wasn't over. Tearing his hamstring was immediately used to strengthen the narrative of Mark being an unfulfilled talent. Commentators presumed that he wasn't training enough, that he didn't have the right mindset or that he wasn't a good professional. It was added to a list of growing fallacies surrounding him from the age of seventeen. The year 2000 had brought Olympic qualification and a world junior title, 2001 brought a sub-ten seconds performance at a World Championships and 2002 brought the title of UK Champion. Selective reasoning dictated that tearing a hamstring at a Commonwealth final while being on the shoulder of the eventual winner proved to some that he was throwing his abilities away, despite the upward trajectory he was clearly on. It was little wonder that Mark yearned for people he could trust and for people to show some respect for his accomplishments and be excited by his potential for the future.

He was nineteen.

What Mark was unaware of was the level of respect his fellow athletes had for him at the time. They knew that the innuendos about his supposed demeanour and background betrayed the real person. His fellow athletes saw him as an enormous threat as an individual and a huge potential ally as a teammate. He elicited feelings of fear or security depending on if you stood opposite or alongside him and not being a huge athletics fan as an athlete, he was both unimpressed by the protocols and grandeur of the sport and unfazed by the grandstanding alpha-male bullshit of some of the big names within it. Due to his treatment in the press, he was slowly becoming indifferent to adversarial comments and uninterested in engaging with people whose opinions he trusted less and less with each passing event.

Conversely, those who earned Mark's trust had quite an ally. He had a raging fire in his stomach wanting to prove a point to those people that they were right to back him. Mark Lewis-Francis was someone who would battle to the death for those that showed faith in him.

PREPARING FOR THE 2003 SEASON WAS A TRIAL OF TRUST. COULD he trust the integrity of his badly torn hamstring? Could he push himself in training, trusting that it simply wouldn't happen again and unravel months of painful physical preparation? Running for Mark had always been his own personal release. Whatever issues were present in the background, the feeling of floating at over 20mph on the back straight at Alexander Stadium with the wind in his face felt like a therapy session. Steve also knew what buttons to press as a coach. He knew Mark enjoyed challenging himself and he'd set targets to hit in training that tested Mark's resilience as well as his performance. Taking on these challenges on the track and spending time in places of extreme discomfort became comfortable to Mark. They became his sanctuary.

While Steve was someone he trusted deeply, 2002 brought the absence of a close male role model in his life into sharp focus as he became a father for the first time. He was forever surrounded by coaches, managers, agents and fellow athletes but there wasn't anyone he could sit down with and talk to about stuff like this. At the same time, he was anxious that many of the officials and management at UK Athletics were already writing him off as not being a serious contender, a feeling exacerbated by missing out on some relay selections. He had lost trust in the press for not giving him a fair hearing despite his accomplishments weighing up favourably against his age and relative inexperience. He had even lost trust in his own body, feeling like his hamstring might tear again at any point. He was always waiting for when he would be let down next.

The World Athletics Championships in Paris became the final straw. He had qualified for these outright by finishing second in the trials but having reached the semi-finals of the 100m and been chosen for the heats of the relays, he was overlooked for selection for the latter stages of the 4 x 100m. Mark watched with solemn pride as his fellow countrymen were chased down by the Americans when gold seemed all but certain. As a part of the team, Mark qualified for a medal so at least his frustrations had a silver lining but even this proved to be false, the team's medals rescinded after the failed drugs test for Chambers. Everywhere Mark looked, it was becoming increasingly impossible to determine what or who to trust.

13

"I trusted these guys with my life's ambitions, which is the same thing as trusting them with my life."

— Darren Campbell

A team isn't created in a boardroom. A high performing sports team is full of people that would take bullets for one another, not bullet points.

In early 2004, the GB Relay squad didn't worry too much about the sexy and modern performance fads that were all the rage at the time. Trust, hard work and application were their foundations and they believed in one another's motives and passions. They were confident in themselves as individuals but were aware of how much more powerful they could be as a truly functioning team. Each man, in his own way and time, had been either directly or inadvertently taught self-reliance by their father figures, whether they were there or not. They had seen the pitfalls of a me-first team environment in previous iterations of the relay setup and now craved sacrifice and discipline on the track to the extent that the coaches would become surrogate father figures, particularly for Mark and Darren. These four men had all struggled with the education system and forged an early distrust of authority figures. Athletics had shown them the value of discipline as schoolboys and now they were realising its value again as adults.

The most conscious aspect to their brotherhood lay in their skin colour. Their shared experiences of racism, both overt and inherent, throughout their lives ensured that everything was always that little bit more difficult for them. There would always be that extra bit of suspicion on them when driving a car late at night. They would always have to be extra mindful of what others thought of them in a way no white person would have to consider. They constantly carried the extra weight of conforming or rebelling against a stereotype. The racism they dealt with was often silent, more insidious than it was obvious.

One of the biggest hurdles to overcome was the almost self-fulfilling, double-sided presumption that by being black athletes they instantly had a chip on their shoulder, that they would encounter a world stacked against them and that they had to act accordingly to combat it. This was both an expectation placed on them by others and something they began to expect of themselves. They found that often, it was much easier to conform to this stereotype. At least it was an easy role to play, one that brought familiar criticisms rather than something unpredictable. Even being athletes, as opposed to doctors, bankers or teachers, meant they were conforming to an acceptable role. 'Of course' they were sprinters; they were black.

Another common trope was the accompanying surprise when they, or any other black athlete, expressed him or herself eloquently and articulately. Even here, there was a choice between a rock and a hard place for black men. When it came to talking, society had its own expectations for black men which left them two options. Conforming to what 'black people sounded like' or expressing themselves in standard elocution like everyone else.

Doing the latter meant being met with a patronising amazement: "*They* speak so well'. The surprise when a black athlete could express themselves in a standard manner followed them often as a standard condescension.

Anna Perez, former communication counselor to US Secretary of State Condoleeza Rice called this out beautifully as:

> "The soft bigotry of low expectations. What they are really saying is that someone is articulate...for a black person."

This was being perpetuated wherever you looked. Former Manchester gang member Darren Campbell not only possessed the education and family upbringing to know right from wrong but to convey his opinions with panache while Jason Gardener in his post-race interviews would pronounce the Queen's English so well that, 'if you closed your eyes', you wouldn't know he was black.

Allyn Condon was the only white athlete in the squad at that time and while he didn't share a skin tone with his teammates, he shared a social bond in coming from Liverpool – a proud city that had struggled for decades with its own deprivation and innuendo based on suppositions of its inhabitants, often strengthened and perpetuated by the media. Sport and politics collided in the attitudes displayed towards the Hillsborough tragedy in 1985 by some of the more shameless sections of the press. Condon knew what it felt like to be stigmatised and blamed for his own circumstances.

The social and emotional background of many of the team was one of having been let down by the system, let down by academia, let down by economic realities, let down by role models, let down by a lack of transparency, let down by performance systems and now with Chambers, even let down by their fellow athletes. To top it all off, they were almost all black and had to deal with the constant expectation that someone would let you down at some point with an outdated attitude, an epithet or an internalised bias. Was there any surprise that they were screaming out for something to put their trust in? They had to prepare to be a team while also competing against one another to qualify. They didn't know if they were going to be selected but they had to be a great teammate regardless. This took a remarkable leap of faith and trust in one another. Considering the scenery and recent events, not bothering was surely the easiest option.

When it came to it, taking the easy option simply wasn't part of their makeup. They'd run towards challenges individually and Marlon, Darren and Jason had been attached to the team for six or seven years, even as long as a decade if their junior days were taken into account. They had bonded like team sport athletes through spending time with one another. They had experienced the joys and the hurt that the relay event could throw at them and they all carried the scars as well as the medals.

Jason Gardener had been through experiences that had ultimately changed his outlook as well as his ability. Dave Lease had made him super-fast and a brilliant racer but when retrospectively appraising his early career, Jason acknowledged that he simply didn't have the experience to put a lot of rounds together on a regular basis. If the definition of insanity was doing the same thing over and over again and getting the same results, the experience of changing to Malcolm Arnold's group was at least a step in a positive direction. Colin Jackson was with Arnold, as well as Alison Curbishley and Mark Foster the swimmer, all based at the University of Bath. Jason couldn't have joined Malcolm Arnold as a young athlete, he simply wouldn't have thrived in that environment at that time. One of his skills was focusing on one thing, then giving that change a chance to grow and see if it made a difference. He was being conditioned a lot more than he ever had before and with Arnold, he trained through muscle soreness where many other coaches would prescribe rest. He became very resilient, ready to go again and again, compensating by losing some weight and strength. His explosive start suffered but his overall ability to run 100m improved. Dave Lease had given Jason the ability to run sub-10 seconds for the 100m and now Malcolm Arnold was giving him the ability to repeat and endure. Jason had also benefited from the experience of experts such as sports scientist Aki Salo, masseur Wayne Gurdlestone and Zara Ford – people he credited with saving his career from the blight of injury. He had learned to take the reins of his own career and look for those that could aid him, to build his own body of work by enlisting the help of people he selected and trusted to give him what he needed.

Darren Campbell had gone the other way, from Malcolm Arnold to Dave Lease. Campbell was one of the more dependable sprinters on the circuit but he'd always watched Jason Gardener's fast start with envy, knowing that it could be a formidable addition to his own repertoire. Lease made Campbell powerful, exceptionally strong, and dynamite from the blocks. Campbell and Gardener, the first half of the relay team at the Athens Olympics, were as heavily invested in each other's pasts as they were to be in their futures. Their career paths were a mirror image.

Campbell's personal experiences had also led him to a point where he was in terms of performance, a ticking time-bomb ready to explode. He had won silver and bronze medals at Olympic Games and World Championships but had punctuated these achievements with years of desolate introspection and disillusionment. His was a life grounded in the fertile soil of violence, crime and danger from the streets of 'Gunchester', meaning that his personal threshold of coping with the red mist of anger was higher than most but that anyone who experienced his wrath did not forget about it in a hurry. When pushed, Campbell's silent stare could shred a person's confidence. Plenty of necks were wound in without a word being said when fixed with the Darren Campbell death stare. Crucially, the relay team that was left standing after the Chambers debacle was full of individuals that were mature enough and had seen enough to not tolerate those meriting such behaviour. Gardener was focused and frankly tired of those that weren't and Devonish was experienced enough to perform at world standard with his eyes closed. He was by this time well along the path to becoming Britain's most medalled athlete and was fired up considering he hadn't been able to run in the 200m. Then there was Mark Lewis-Francis.

Even at the tender age of twenty, there was little tenderness left in Lewis-Francis's attitude on track. His rise to featuring as a potential relay star in the Olympics had all happened within three years. Experiences that many athletes would have spent decades accumulating had happened to him in a flash. He had dealt with overachievement in qualifying for Sydney, winning a World Junior title and with the ups and downs of injury all with the perpetual buzzing of commentators' doubts in the background. Mark's body might have been approaching his twenty-first year but his experiences rivalled those finishing their careers. While many of his social peers were choosing whether to continue apprenticeships or gently negotiating career leaps from graduates to employees, Mark's career was already grinding to a halt if you listened to the prevailing narrative around him. When Jason, Darren and Marlon put their trust in him, he was beside himself. He wanted to invest his energy in people who believed in him. Bringing everyone together was the key and he wanted to be a part of that.

The team now trusted one another and had a large bank of experience to call upon. What had historically let the British team down in competition was simple execution. Rather than facilitate the smooth progress of the baton around the track, the constituent parts of the team would cough and splutter at crucial points, building to failure rather than success.

No matter how much trust and belief the team had, they were still going to have to cope with the lowly, unfamiliar process of qualifying for the Games. For superstar sprinters, this was not the done thing. It was unseemly for them, even a bit embarrassing, but there was a positive side effect. They had an unusual opportunity to properly hone the 0.8 second flash of arms and steel of the relay changeover. They got to get their reps in in real time, under the very real pressure of having to qualify against real opposition, all under the full glare of an audience.

The changeover is not a one size fits all skill. Some are 'pushers' of the baton, some are 'slappers-down'. Some like it early, others late. Some like it in the left hand, others – as Usain Bolt would mention to Marlon – in their right. Stealing precious milliseconds in a symphony of sprinting would only happen if they wrote a script that could be agreed upon and rehearsed. Attempting to refine this crucial discipline when the team would only know its constituent parts a few days prior was in retrospect, inviting failure upon itself. If the baton handover was approached as a closed and specific skill - like Tiger Woods's stance while driving from the tee or Jonny Wilkinson's metronomic kicking technique – it would create a wider margin for success. Often making something complex simple is easy but bringing sophistication and complexity to something simple is hard. A decision was made by the athletes themselves to make the changeover a forensic skill.

There was common sense and a successful precedent behind this approach. Darren and Marlon, in their baton exchange at the end of the back straight in Paris the previous summer, had eaten up yards on the American Darvis Patton and handed Dwain Chambers a decent lead before Chambers had run into a moral cul-de-sac instead of to the top of the podium. There was also the romantic reminiscence of Jason Gardener practicing his relay exchanges with his coach in his teenage years, a practice grounded at the time in quaint overoptimism that he would need that skill someday. As fate would have it, not only would he benefit from those childhood changeovers but the others would too. Plenty of Great Britain relay teams had demonstrated that poor changeovers could result in a royal mess. Perhaps the opposite was also true and fantastic changeovers could yield success, particularly if the orthodox approach was to just safely hand the baton on rather than do it as smoothly as possible. The idea of turning a weakness into a strength is not new and seems like an obvious track to take but it's the sort of endeavour that sounds great on paper or on the boardroom Powerpoint, but making it a reality requires on the ground focus, unity and sheer bloodyminded practice.

THE RELAY TEAM HAD HISTORICALLY BEEN A PLACE WHERE athletes were comfortable. This was the environment that Perks, Devonish, Campbell and Gardener had been introduced to initially. There had been few repercussions for lateness or tardiness and the meetings and practices themselves had a slightly 'feet up and smile' atmosphere as opposed to the drive and focus that typified each athlete's individual sessions. There was always lots of banter and leg-pulling in such a high testosterone environment but their horseplay wasn't grounded in a dynasty of champions or a legacy of success. Athletes within the British relay team sometimes had a misplaced gold-medal mentality even when failing to get out of the semi-finals. The mocking and chat could be ruthless and if an athlete failed to hold their own socially, they would sometimes wither away. While often cruel, the off-track repartee built resilience and strong spines as much as the experiences on-track. After all, once you were in the holding pen prior to the race at the Olympic Games, the other teams were going to climb into you.

Yet this was all wrong. As most successful sportspeople know, the ones with the most to shout about are often the ones that raise their voices the least. Bravado can mask insecurity. In sport, whether as an athlete or a coach, a supremely confident front can stem from an inadequacy of self-awareness, achievement or conviction.

The days of using a façade of strength and arrogance needed to be consigned to history for the relay team to thrive. The team had to be built on a confidence that had its root in the certainty of its own performance, not who was the wittiest or who demonstrated the strongest alpha presence. Even the performance variables themselves needed to be broken down and dissected. The athletes found that despite best intentions, the management could get into the athletes' heads too much at times. In a quest to boost confidence or give a gentle prod, giving stats and facts could inadvertently throw people off if, for instance, the wind was different or if the occasion drove up the adrenaline higher than normal. The feeling between the two athletes exchanging the baton could affect timings and the positions of the floor checkmarks could change the dynamics. Coaches' third-party appraisals could cause problems and mistiming when for the athletes themselves, the art of the movement was as important as the science. Only through practicing did all these factors become apparent. The mentality of the constituent athletes within the wider relay group was changing the more they were learning about themselves as cogs within a machine.

Months before, they had been waiting for team members to arrive late carrying fast food and laughing. Now when any of the team said "bring it in" or snapped their fingers, each athlete listened because they respected what anyone had to say, ready to learn and develop. The psychological landscape had changed entirely. The British relay team was now a place of mutual respect and constant learning. The physiological aspect was locked in, with all athletes having produced fast times and won medals over the previous season, breeding an emotional confidence.

On leg one there was Jason Gardener, the perfect first leg runner with a blistering start and the decades-long familiarity of handling a baton at speed. Jason was highly motivated to be back in the team and was thriving within the fertile ground of critical analysis and perfectionism that he'd help to cultivate.

Darren Campbell, fresh from being a whisker away from being World 100m Champion, was the steam train on the back straight. Darren had once been the cause of failure for the relay team, had seen it flounder numerous other times and was in no mood to waste his time investing energy in a cause that wasn't going to shock the world.

Marlon Devonish had become arguably the best bend runner in the world and one of the most highly skilled technical baton exchangers. His attitude and composure had stayed constant and true through many successes and failures over the years and as much as he enjoyed being a dependable component of a team, he'd recently been greatly disappointed by the missed open goal of Paris where he had played his part in providing a strong lead only for it to disappear.

Mark Lewis-Francis was ambitious and emotive on the last leg. For this team at this time he was the perfect anchor runner, any element of fear drowned out by his animalistic urge to succeed. Many young athletes would have shrunk standing on the home straight of an Olympic final with the likes of Maurice Greene in the next lane, their psychological war lost before it had begun. Mark wanted to be there, looking into the lion's jaw, in a position where he could ram a few words down a few people's necks and in his own words ensure that,

> "Those who were calling you 'ABC' are now applauding you on tv."

He would soon get his opportunity.

14

20 WEEKS TO GO
ATHENS 2004

Jason Gardener was looking at a scan. It was February 2004, there were two weeks to go before the World Indoor Championships at the Budapest Sports Arena and he had just learned he needed a hernia operation. Immediately.

While he'd been in pain for a few weeks, he'd been running ridiculously quickly in training and had recently equalled his own European 60m record in competition. Jason felt that he was in shape to be World Champion. At one of Malcolm Arnold's sessions, he warmed up slowly but the pain was just as bad as it ever had been. Cautiously, carefully, he tiptoed his way along the familiar line between warming up enough to perform at the required intensity and exacerbating what was clearly some sort of abdominal injury. Running just a little quicker with each warm up repetition, he decided to attempt the session. Arnold was never one to show emotion. He told Jason to run through the timing gates over and over again. After around five or six runs the pain was increasing, necessitating constant on track physio from Chris Price, but while he couldn't ignore his body screaming at him to stop, the times were dropping significantly with each subsequent effort. Jason had got his body to a point where he didn't need to make a maximal effort to run well. He was growing in confidence, feeling that he could perform well enough to win with a different, more conservative approach to the past.

Jason needed surgery, but here was an opportunity to become a World Champion. He had evidence that he could perform to the level required to win and that his body could stand up to more prolonged efforts that would be needed at the championships. He delayed the surgery and kept his injury quiet. He didn't want anyone to know he was hurt. Arnold told him to show ruthlessness in the face of adversity saying, "You go to fucking win – no fucking around". When he won that race, becoming World Indoor 60m Champion while knowing that he needed a double hernia operation, he proved to himself that he had the mental toughness to triumph when not everything was going to plan.

Meanwhile, Mark Lewis-Francis was becoming numb to the sport of track and field. His career seemed to be playing out as a big game of snakes and ladders, with the ladders not only coming infrequently, but not climbing as high as he'd like. He was merely twenty years of age at this point but he was already feeling like a jaded professional.

Going into the 2004 season, he decided to attack the air of apathy that was settling around him. Rather than be indifferent, he settled on getting angry to prove a point to his detractors as well as to himself. This year was an Olympic year and there were places up for grabs. He'd let the last Games go by in what he'd thought was an intelligent move and been castigated for it. He wasn't going to let another Games go by. He was going to get to whatever start line he needed to get to and when he got there, he just wanted to eat the track.

Dwain Chambers' ban worked in Mark's favour as he would be one of the primary candidates to run the anchor leg for the Olympic relay team. While there would be insinuations of promotion by default, he'd now been a relay reserve twice in situations where he had qualified for the championships outright as an individual athlete. Even though he sometimes felt like the black sheep in a wider squad including Darren, Jason and Marlon, along with Dwayne Grant, Nick Smith, Chris Lambert and Christian Malcolm, Mark knew his performances that season warranted selection. He deserved to be there.

Despite being a successful athlete, Mark didn't consider himself a huge track and field fan. He loved the sport but didn't obsess over the performances of others or bury his head in statistics and analysis like many of his contemporaries. Even still, it was impossible not to be aware of the stellar recent history of British sprinting. His predecessors in the British vest included heavyweights such as Linford Christie, John Regis, Colin Jackson and Tony Jarrett. Over the years, it was generally accepted that London-based athletes had received a leg up when it came to selection, even in a sport as theoretically meritocratic as track and field. London had always provided the bulk of the UK team with athletes such as Christie, Regis and Jarrett along with John Ridgeon and Roger Black, all either from London or based there. The athletes in the 4 x 100m relay team in 2004 were drawn from a much wider catchment area, with Bath (Jason), Manchester (Darren), Coventry (Marlon) and Birmingham (Mark) supplemented by a supporting cast from Scotland (Smith) and South Wales (Malcolm). Even though selectors were clearly looking further afield, the athletes had felt the need to overstate their cases in their younger years in order to gain selection over competitors from more convenient locations as far as training, selection and coaching were concerned. If you wanted to be selected from Scotland, you'd need to be much, much quicker than the kid from Streatham. The walls that needed to be scaled for success were sometimes supported by the Ordnance Survey.

The Olympic Trials held at SportCity, Manchester would decide who would qualify for the Athens Games. Many of the athletes had already posted Olympic qualifying times and with the discretionary vote of the selectors playing a part in selection, finishing in the top two was paramount in order to guarantee a spot in Greece. The trials were not held within the glorious surroundings of the soon-to-be Etihad Stadium but next door in what had been the warm-up track for the Commonwealth Games, now a 7,000-capacity stadium in its own right. The athletes called the rarely-used track 'sponge-like' and 'slow', not ideal when powerful sprinters are hoping to impress with fast times.

Trials are always a significant hurdle for the realisation of an athlete's dream. While most fans see the Olympic Games as where dreams are realised, without turning up in the right condition to earn your plane ticket, you might as well keep dreaming. You need to be preparing to peak at the Olympics but if you get it wrong at trials, you won't be peaking for anything at all.

These trials were a knife-edge moment for many of those lining up. Jason had become an expert in realpolitik and the skills of managing up as much as he had become an expert in flat speed since the previous Olympic Games. The cliche of needing to let his actions on the track do the talking was in this instance, not a cliche at all. He'd made his points eloquently enough in street clothes, now he needed to do the same in his spikes. Mark had qualified for Sydney 2000 but had decided not to go in service of the big picture. Now was the time to paint his masterpiece but if he forgot his brush, he'd have missed an earlier Olympic opportunity for no reason at all. Darren had a simpler motivation. He was older and his time was running out. In all likelihood, these would be his last games.

For the athletes, the ten minutes of waiting to run and the ten seconds or so of the race were purely transactional. Their effort, preparation and performance for a place on the plane. While they all wanted to run fast, all that mattered to those on the start line were the placings at the end of the race, irrespective of time, who they beat or how well they ran. While those watching could feel the drama, the competitors were there to do a job.

The men's 100m saw Jason Gardener win with Darren Campbell second and Mark Lewis-Francis third, the very same three athletes that had stood on the podium a year previously, albeit in different positions. They all finished within a hundredth of a second of one another and they would all be going to Athens. Mark wouldn't be giving up his spot this time.

Mark had tremendous respect for his fellow sprinters in the UK, especially Gardener, Campbell, Malcolm and Devonish. Darren and Mark had clicked as friends as well as rivals, always indulging in a lot of leg-pulling. Having grown up in the Midlands, he knew the name Marlon Devonish before ever meeting or competing with him and Jason Gardener was an ever-present name and an ever-present threat. Mark realised that he could be involved in a relay team full of athletes that he had a very, very high regard for. The prospect excited him.

Soon to become an Olympian, Mark considered his path to this point. He'd personally overcome so many barriers to become a success. Even though athletics didn't require much gear to participate, the guys had all overcome significant friction to even make it to training sessions. Three bus journeys didn't seem too appealing in the bleak midwinter, particularly when your friends were just going to hang out, make music or mischief and mess about together. Mark felt that his experiences in athletics gave him an edge over other people and he recognised similar traits in his teammates. They had all persisted with the sport through painful training and the highs and lows of racing. They'd experienced financial, familial and social pressures that could easily have stopped them from running, from when they were teenagers to experienced professionals. They had succeeded despite, not because of many things.

THE PREVIOUS LAISSEZ-FAIRE ATTITUDE TO THE RELAY EVENT HAD time and again culminated in a laissez-faire end product. The relays used to be a lot of fun. People used to mess around a bit. There were jokes and relaxed practices, never involving the stress of full race conditions and timings. Jason Gardener had walked away after his experiences in Annecy and had he raised his voice to pop the party balloon and advocate a more stringent attitude at that time, he may well have been in the minority. This had changed. The team were now earnest and solemn in their determination to succeed. Darren had jumped over many personal hurdles since his stellar year in 2000, demonstrating incredible mental and physical fortitude to climb back to the top of the sport at the Manchester Commonwealth games. It was tough to tolerate lackadaisical attitudes after experiencing firsthand where focus and fortitude could take you. Why should he climb out of his own hole only to have others merrily dig one for him?

By now, Marlon had lived through all the possible successes and problems, had seen all the mistakes, strategies and performance fads come and go. He had the experience and reference points to see a potential hazard coming over the horizon. He was as tired as the others of seeing mistakes costing titles and was in no mood to allow himself to be in an environment where standards weren't reflective of the performances required for success.

These athletes had all lost medals, dreams and money due to the attitudes of others. While the 2003 medal had been lost through the cheating of one athlete, Jason, Marlon and Darren had learned that anyone not showing respect and dedication to a team was in some way cheating.

In winning the British title, Jason's performances ensured he was heading to Athens but he was still recovering from a double hernia operation and had run the Olympic trials at 80% effort. He was also carrying a heavy secret. If selected for the relay team in Athens, he would be holding the baton with a fully broken wrist. Both he and the medical team decided that the pain was manageable and as it wouldn't impact his running, this information would not be shared with the coaches or the athletes. Carrying the baton would be searingly painful but wouldn't hurt as much as watching the Olympics on television.

Marlon had qualified solely for the relay at this Olympics and wouldn't be involved in any individual event. Once again he had overtrained and suffered a hamstring injury. While this was a lesson Marlon struggled to learn, the injury kept him off his feet and by the time they arrived at the pre-Games holding camp in Cyprus he was healthy, fresh and absolutely flying. He hadn't raced much that season due to his injury and was therefore both hungry to compete and completely unaffected by fatigue. Many of his peers on the team were commenting that they had never seen him run so well, or so quickly. Marlon acknowledged their compliment while also biting his lip in frustration that he was probably not going to figure in any individual event. In any case, it made him even more determined that the relay be a success and woe betide anyone who stood in the way.

The team's inward focus was probably for the best given that there was an extraordinary amount of bad press around the British team leading into the Games. Bad press about Dwain Chambers, about losing the Paris silver medal, negativity about the history of the British relay team and even some scathing articles written regarding the discrepancy between the financial investment in the team and the yield of medals. While the criticism hurt, many of these pieces were justified and expectations going into Athens were not high. Paula Radcliffe and Kelly Holmes were touted as potential outsiders for medals and that was about it. There were many 'cost-of-pounds-per-medal' graphics appearing in the sports pages and the narrative was of a failing team becoming a growing black hole of lottery funding and giving nothing back in return. There was a distinctly underdog feel to the team at its pre-Olympic holding camp in Paphos, Cyprus.

Cyprus was so hot that training timetables were dictated by the waxing and waning of the temperature. Athletes used to setting their own individual schedules were wisely encouraged to limit their training to between 9:30am and 11:30am and the late afternoon once the heat had subsided. It prepared the athletes for the conditions in Athens but as with many pre-competition camps, collecting all the athletes together in one team before an assault on the Games felt more like an administrative exercise than best practice for acclimatisation. Many of the world's best athletes would not attend their own teams' holding camps, preferring to trust their own instincts and habits than be forced to follow a daily plan of someone else's making. The days were long, with plenty of food, too much heat and not a small amount of boredom. Paphos was a beautiful setting for a team escape but the looming spectre of the world's biggest sporting event made sightseeing an unnecessary frivolity.

A ten-year deal had been signed between the British Olympic Association and the Cyprus Tourism Association to create the Team GB training base, including the construction of a new Olympic 50-metre pool and a brand-new running track. This deal ensured that the team would hold a camp to justify the spend. The England Rugby team had won the Rugby World Cup twelve months previously based on a no-stone-left-unturned philosophy which became a precursor for the soon-to-be famous, later infamous marginal gains concept and the British Olympic team was similarly resource-rich, dripping with money, expertise and top-class facilities. Sadly however, this emphasis on the icing and not the cake meant that while there were the trappings of high performance, what the team didn't have was a multitude of athletes able to dominate the world stage in a variety of events in Athens. There was pressure on the Team GB administrators to produce medals and pressure on the athletes to perform but these expectations were not rooted in reality. Even a casual glimpse at world standards in the weeks prior to the Games would have clearly indicated a lean Olympics for the Great Britain and Northern Ireland team.

The intention of the camp was to simulate the experience of the Games and enable everyone to become familiar with the structure of the team environment prior to arriving in Athens. It would also negate the effects of jet lag and heat on the athletes. There would be time to familiarise with management processes, transport logistics, accommodation specifics and enable the development of core working relationships between coaches and athletes, as well as between performance directors and the support staff.

None of this was necessarily going to make an athlete run any faster.

The unpalatable truth for those signing the cheques was that it was more of a dry run for the support staff than it was for the athletes. Many athletes openly grumbled about having to adhere to unfamiliar and untried daily timetables organised by personnel who had limited interaction with them for forty-seven of the forty-eight month Olympic cycle. Why interrupt your familiar routine for any longer than you had to?

Darren was familiar with external processes interrupting his best laid plans. At Sydney 2000, his coach Linford Christie was denied team accreditation to enter the athlete area, depriving him of his most important supporter right when he needed him. For Darren, the Cyprus holding camp was just something that had to be done.

It did provide some of the athletes with an opportunity to sharpen up before heading to the Games and Marlon Devonish was feeling like he'd been honed to a point. He hadn't yet enjoyed the opportunity to post a big performance in a race but there was significant enthusiasm among the British athletes about his form at the holding camp. Finishing outside the medals at the Olympic trials and being selected for the team late gave him no time to build any emotion or overthink. There was only the time to turn up and demonstrate his quality.

Just getting to an Olympic Games is a phenomenal achievement. You are there to compete with the cream of the sporting world, the pinnacle of human physical performance. Becoming an Olympian begets a family legacy, where great-grandchildren are told that their relative went to the Olympics. While being a champion is the ultimate goal, even to make it to a Games an achievement and not only that, it's part of the ethos of the Olympics. Pierre de Coubertin, the man that revived the Olympic Games, said that,

> "The important thing in life is not the triumph but the struggle, the essential thing is not to have conquered but to have fought well."

For those that have battled to qualify, have no medal expectations and are just pleased to be there, the Olympics are a parallel dimension, a Las Vegas/World Cup/Mardi Gras/Glastonbury bizarro fortnight where usually under-the-radar athletes are treated like superstars. Good times, easy attitudes and intense experiences are squeezed into an Olympic Village the size of a small university campus for two weeks. For those that fancy it, parties, concerts and hedonistic behaviour are merely a message or a swipe away. Teams of the fittest, most sculpted athletes from around the world share the same communal areas, organise events together and for many, enjoy a level of multinational promiscuity unseen since the days of Woodstock. The Olympic Games are a free plane ride to an exotic location with hundreds of friends and colleagues in tow, free accommodation, food, sunshine, sex and sangria included, all while being feted by the world as a star. It can be the best holiday you'll ever have, watching some of the world's greatest athletes do their thing. If you're not there explicitly to win, the Olympics can be a lot of fun.

For those who fancy a podium finish, this is all a distraction best ignored. The Olympics are only truly that much fun for those that know deep down that not only are they not going to win, but there is a very real chance that they will never attend another. Those two weeks need to be seized, enjoyed and savoured before they vanish, like last night's fever dream. For the best athletes, the hedonism begins only when the competition ends, the partying tasting all the sweeter for the four years' worth of stoic discipline and sacrifice being capped with a medal, preferably gold.

The Olympic Games can be amazing fun. How much fun depends on how much you want to win.

THE DYNAMIC WITHIN THE RELAY TEAM HAD BECOME unrecognisable in four years. The management at Sydney 2000 had to deal with and attempt to manage a group of large egos, all wanting to be respected and treated as winners even when there was no guarantee of a place, let alone a medal. There was no real team. Every member wanted to be an individual first and the arrogance and sense of entitlement which filtered through the team ultimately bit back hard. Four years later, the team had been humbled many times. They were forced to rebuild slowly over months and years, rising to a crescendo in Paris with a World silver medal, only to see this achievement snatched from them with a failed urine sample. The team were now quiet and solemn in their preparation where their predecessors had been loud and insincere. In having to achieve qualification for the Athens Games from the lowly ranking of fifteenth in the world, they also had learned to value the importance of a culture of repetition and rehearsal. They felt that they had the ability - they'd been in the mix for a gold medal in Paris - but they had no credibility. They knew that this had to be earned by them and them alone.

Darren, Mark and Jason had qualified for the individual 100m at the Athens Olympic Games, Darren going out in the first round and the latter two falling in the semi-finals. Jason and Mark's solo Olympic dreams were over once again. Darren had qualified for the 200m with Christian Malcolm and Chris Lambert but with a hamstring tear hampering his preparation, failed to replicate his silver medal performance in Sydney and similarly fell at the semi-final hurdle. There was no British involvement in any of the men's sprint finals.

Given how the team were faltering individually, a cohesive assault on the relay event seemed unlikely. Nevertheless, it was all they had left.

The journey to Athens had been long and arduous. The team had battled for everything and even when they'd overcome what was in front of them, they'd contrived to trip themselves up. The four athletes, along with Steve Perks and Aki Salo, collected together all these failures and identified common themes, opportunities and lessons to be learnt. They had forensically broken down the demands of the event and micro-planned each constituent aspect but there was a wider, more global lesson that they'd learned. They knew about themselves as people.

Applying true introspection and honesty when looking to better yourself is not easy. It means admitting weakness and relinquishing ego, traits not normally associated with burly, alpha-male, world-class sprinters. The four athletes were in different stages of their career but they were as people, unified in giving each other their full support. There was no energy wasted through ego or politics as there had been in Sydney, no over-competitive grandstanding between the four or any notion of hierarchical dominance within the group. They knew their opponents well but they had come to learn more about themselves, none more so than Darren Campbell.

Darren was at a point in his career where his experiences, hunger, maturity and knowledge had reached a crest just before age would take his physical capacities away from him. He was in the performance sweet-spot of peaking physically, mentally and in terms of experience but had failed to qualify for the finals in both individual sprint events. Despite his qualities aligning at the right time, Darren had underperformed hugely, mainly because his hamstring would not allow him to fully express his speed, a simple reason that many would regard as an excuse. He was desperate because he knew that he was at his last Olympic Games and frustrated because he was unable to do himself justice. He spoke with his doctor, his team-mates in the relay and his trusted support team, including members of his old Manchester crew who had made the journey to support him. The thought of discreetly flying home was certainly on the cards.

BBC Sport's daily Olympic television coverage included multiple Olympic champion Michael Johnson as a guest. As a part of the broadcast, the presenters and commentators would discuss and dissect recent events as well as provide opinion and insight into the events to come. Upon discussing the British team's performance in the sprint events and the relay to come, Johnson poured cold water on the idea of Darren being injured as a reason for underperformance. He questioned the veracity of his story, essentially calling him a faker. A narrative suddenly exploded through the media channels that one of the world's greatest ever athletes was calling out one of Britain's greatest ever athletes for being a fraud. This led to the UK Athletics doctor Bryan English offering medical evidence to settle the story and take air out of what was a potentially damaging and inaccurate declaration to the millions of watching armchair fans. Johnson was a highly respected athlete whose voice people took seriously and there was a serious possibility that his interpretation would become accepted fact.

This placed Campbell in a precarious situation. If he left the Olympics, he would now in the public's eyes lend credence to Johnson's version of events. He would be tarnished as a quitter, despite him having a legitimate reason to leave the Games. Darren was furious and determined to do his talking on the track, even if his hamstring would decide whether he would be able to prove his point.

In the course of the situation playing out, one of his hometown friends from Manchester, Lynx, managed to convince him to let off some steam by attending an open-air nightclub party held by MTV. The way he saw it, if his Olympics were over, he might as well spend some time enjoying himself and if his Olympics had a final coda, it would do him good to get out of the apartment and stretch his legs for a few hours. As fate would have it, among the many celebrities at the party was Michael Johnson. Campbell accosted his accuser immediately, demanding to know whether he had intended to call him a faker in front of a nationwide audience. When Johnson turned his back to Campbell, he was enraged. Only the timely intervention of Lynx prevented things coming to blows. Leaving the party that night, Campbell resolved to stay at the Olympics and ram a few words down a few people's throats.

WHILE DARREN AND MARK WERE BOTH CHOMPING AT THE BIT TO prove their detractors wrong, the athletes had no idea who was likely to be selected for the relay. Coaches Steve Perks and Graham Knight had given nothing away and had presumably been waiting for the 200m to be over before deciding the final makeup of the team. With the British involvement in the 200m ending early, time was on their side. Darren took the lead on behalf of the athletes, stating a consensus that the team needed to know who was in and who was out early. The notion of the athletes taking ownership was actually occurring and while the coaches had control over selection, order and strategy, the athletes were finally owning their own preparation. Here was the integrated performance model that everyone talked about but never before enacted.

Led by Darren, the athletes held a meeting with the coaches to do two things; to finalise selection and for all the athletes to look one another in the eye to see who was ready to put everything on the line and who was not. In the carnival atmosphere of the Olympic Village, tranquility and privacy were at a premium and the only place they could find to meet was a dark, windowless boiler room in the unfinished apartment complex, full of boxes, lined with concrete and with silver foil and bare pipes running along the roofs. The athletes and coaches filed into this inauspicious venue and began to talk. The coaches named the chosen four in their running order and the die was cast. This could have signalled the end of the meeting but for the athletes, it was the start of things. The team held their own discussion.

The team dynamics engendered in the group were revealed in how the athletes spoke about one another in that boiler room. Marlon or Jason would say, "I know Darren and he would/wouldn't..." Darren or Mark would say "Jason will give us this..." It was a team considering itself with complete honesty, integrity and transparency. The non-selected athletes showed phenomenal integrity and selflessness by pledging their unwavering support to those that had been selected. Whatever was to come next, the journey that they all had been on had led them to the point that they were now in sync, unified as a team. Any friction or animosity within the team had previously been ignored for fear of rattling the cage but now the team was declaring its vulnerabilities and weaknesses to itself openly and candidly. There was also a feeling of warmth and solidarity towards Christian Malcolm, who had fallen ill at the Olympics and was unable to be even considered for the relay. Christian was not only popular and jovial, he was an exceptionally capable member of the team.

Darren stated openly that he thought his hamstring might be vulnerable to tearing again if he ran maximally and that he could step aside. The team's response was that him running maximally was worth the risk and that they would take the chance to have a fully firing Darren Campbell on their side. Marlon hadn't run many races and hadn't proved his form but the team had seen him in practice and knew they could depend on him. When Mark heard his name as the anchor runner, he struggled to hold back the tears. He was desperate to phone home and relay the good news to his family but in the days before FaceTime and Zoom, overseas calls were extortionately expensive so he decided against it.

It was an emotional room as the guys learned truly how they felt about each other and realised the confidence that they had in one another. Mark understood that he was the rookie in the team, but while he was expecting to feed off of the others, he realised that they fed off of him. They wanted his gnarly, brute attitude to manifest itself on the last leg, to turn his aggression and fearlessness up to eleven. Mark could be the antithesis of the archetypal nervous last leg runner bereft of confidence and easily manipulated by the big guns. More experienced athletes than him had faltered in that role but he didn't have the burden of prior personal failure there. Being selected and realising how he was regarded by his teammates fuelled him and gave them all the belief that they could do something.

On paper the British team didn't look great in comparison to the Americans who were swaggering through the individual sprint events, sweeping up all the medals in the 200m and taking gold and bronze in the 100m. Still, they knew they were better than the evidence suggested and swore to one another that they would give their all. They believed they could win, even if no one else did.

The relay heats were held later in the evening on 27th August 2004. Darren's hamstring had had a couple of days of complete rest after the 200m and Jason and Mark had been able to rest for almost a week since the 100m. They were drawn in lane 2 in the semi-finals with the Americans on their outside. They knew that they had the calibre to proceed to the final but having to run the tighter inside lane coupled with meeting the favourites in the heats seeded some doubt in their minds. Darren had been injured, Mark was feeling a bit jaded and wasn't the athlete he usually was, Jason was only a few months from a serious hernia operation and Marlon had no competitive reps under his belt. There was no evidence of any true speed to challenge the lightning times of the Americans. What they lacked in speed they would make up for in team spirit, resilience and camaraderie.

Britain qualified second behind the Americans but the performance was shambolic. There were nerves, miscues and the changeovers didn't look like something honed through hours of rehearsal. They looked about as polished as a staff quartet at a school sports day. The chain reaction of clumsiness from the first changeover onwards culminated in Mark going out hard and early, only just getting back into the zone to make a legal changeover. The flow from one athlete to the next was so bad that when Aki Salo showed them the tape afterwards, they didn't know whether to laugh or grimace. Despite flirting with catastrophe, they ran a time of 38.53 seconds while closely resembling four strangers clumsily exchanging a hot potato so there was something to work with here. They reconvened in the boiler room, this time with Aki Salo and his videotapes.

Coach Steve Perks reframed what had happened. Yes, the performance was rusty, but he saw many mitigating circumstances. They were on a tight inside lane, with a pole vault bed placed unnervingly close to the track between two of the changeovers. The fact that they qualified second placed and were given lane three for the final would make things easier. The heat performance was good enough to get to the final but by their new standards, wasn't good enough. The bar had been raised. They would have been satisfied with that performance a few years prior as a semi-final but now their own expectations had raised considerably. They were chasing a perfect race.

One decision had been a masterstroke. Using the same team in the semi-final and the final ensured that there would be one more rehearsal (if they qualified) as a four and also focused each athlete on the here and now. Had the team been changed for the final, there would have been no lessons learnt from the semi-final and the dynamic between the four would have to adapt again. As it happened, the members of the relay team that hadn't been selected had more time to deal with the disappointment and had a chance to either support the team or disappear from view. The reserves supported them brilliantly. Upon reviewing the tapes, the truth of the semi-final performance was that there was speed and smoothness in parts but everything was a little forced and quick. The team needed to slow the process down a bit and trust their training.

Sitting down and watching their footage over and over, it became evident that many of their mistakes were based on exuberance. The training didn't come out in the baton exchanges, the team dynamic looked a little rusty and the athletes were not quite on the same wavelength. In the claustrophobic, cramped boiler room, all crowded around a small television, the four of them looked at one another knowing that if they could tidy up the changeovers and get their timings right, they would be dangerous. The penny dropped by looking at the mistakes.

The input of Aki Salo was key to the strategic assessment of the relay. Salo had been brought in by Graham Knight in order to biomechanically break down the key aspects of the performances. He would often give the athletes a videotape of the relay practices and there was plenty to be learnt from his data analysis. The athletes thought he was exceptional throughout but one afternoon at the Paphos training camp weeks stood out. A changeover between Marlon and Mark in a session in Paphos was clocked and verified as the quickest box-to-box baton handover Aki Salo had ever recorded by any team. This was significant because unlike a hole-in-one golf shot or a full-court "Hail Mary" basketball bucket, you didn't simply fluke into a record changeover at Olympic relay level. Perks, Knight and Salo then had to decide what to do with this information.

They decided to deprive the athletes of this snippet of knowledge, feeling it would be a distraction which might lead to over-excitement within the team. In any case, this level of mastery appeared completely impossible considering what had been displayed in the semi-final performance. The team inadvertently created its own rope-a-dope moment, cloaking their surgical dexterity with clumsiness.

The press became very edgy and nervous, thinking the GB team was once again not prepared. The television pundits scrutinised Marlon and Mark's changeover very closely at the end of the box, astonished at how close it was to being a disqualification and how messy it all looked. They were right to scrutinise those aspects of the performance; as soon as the race had ended, Mark's first question to Marlon was, "Did we change that in the box?"

The team was being written off in some circles before the final. Dwain's name was brought up again. Mark was fulfilling expectations of being unable to fulfil his promise. Some said the team looked overweight and undertrained and while Marlon looked in shape, he hadn't competed in months. Jason had failed to take his chance in the 100m and when all was said and done, was only a 60m runner anyway. Darren was either injured or a faker and unable to focus due to being in the middle of a spat with Michael Johnson. His compatriots on the USA team would have seen the British performance in the semi-final and thought, 'those guys are a complete mess'. There didn't appear to be any threat coming from the Brits.

On Sunday August 22nd, American Justin Gatlin was crowned Olympic 100m Champion. Fellow American Maurice Greene claimed bronze with American Shaun Crawford edged out of the medals in fourth. Three of the top four finishers in the men's 100m final all came from the USA. Worryingly for their relay rivals, not only did they all break the ten seconds barrier; they all ran below 9.90.

Four days later, the USA enjoyed a clean sweep of all the medals in the 200m with Shaun Crawford becoming Olympic Champion in a blistering 19.79 seconds, Bernard Williams taking second and Justin Gatlin finishing third. All three came close to breaking the twenty-second barrier for the 200m.

This level of dominance was unheard of. The American team had never been so strong, so consistent or so stacked with talent. They would conceivably have to relegate an individual medal winner to a relay team reserve. Despite any notions of brotherhood, teamwork and belief from the British foursome, these superlative American performances cemented one fact: the men's 4 x 100m relay final was a foregone conclusion.

15

AUGUST 28TH 2004

> "The media crucified us before the final. It was going to be a failure. They kept bringing Dwain up, and how Mark had failed to fulfil his promise. Some of us were overweight and undertrained, I had failed to take my chance in the 100m and was only really a good 60m runner anyway. We were written off already and worse than that, the stories about how we were going to fail were probably already written."
>
> — Jason Gardener

By now, the British relay team had surely uncovered every mistake that it was possible to make.

To be able to relinquish egos and appraise a very poor semi-final performance was typical of a group of individuals that were now able to use some introspection. Years of practice and experience in learning from their mistakes had brought them closer not just as a functioning team, but as people. They felt an intuition when it came to the changeovers. The mistakes in the semi-final had come as a surprise, for they had been very detailed in training sessions, but now mistakes were there to be learnt from.

They had managed to unearth every conceivable means of prizing defeat from the jaws of success in the relay event and now, there was nothing that could surprise them. Now that they knew the pitfalls and how fast their poor performance was, they just had to make their adjustments in a cool, professional, pragmatic manner. Then they might just shock the world.

On a personal level, there was complete psychological safety in this team. Everyone knew everything about the other and felt secure in contributing towards one other's ambitions. The four athletes were the definition of a cohesive unit, all on the same page and confident that they could now do their abilities justice. They felt a collective ownership of whatever outcome lay ahead, whether they'd be celebrating or commiserating. As people, they had come to trust, admire and even like one another over the years, as rivals and as brothers in arms. They had engendered a perfect combination of respect, trust and faith in one another.

The problem was, the Americans were far quicker than them. The standards needed to achieve qualification for the American team far exceeded any other nation on earth given that the United States had athletes capable of running 9.80 seconds for the 100m incapable of qualifying for their team. To the outside world, there was no contest here.

THE DAYS LEADING UP TO THE RACE WERE A COMPLETE antithesis of the dysfunction in Sydney four years prior. The entire team including the non-selected athletes, met, ate, and socialised together as a squad in the days leading up to the relay. They prepared together for the unexpected. They checked each other's spare spikes and apparel, prepared timetables and contingencies for what happened if they missed the bus or if there was a problem. They helped each other to relax and to focus on the task ahead. Each cog in the machine was checking that the other had enough oil.

The final was set for late evening. The day had been broken up by a few naps and some gentle walking around the Olympic Village. After a late lunch, they had a meeting before the final relay practice at the warm up track.

When the British team arrived at the Athens games, the sight that awaited them at the warm up track was both comic and worrying. Firstly, there was no shade to speak of around the track to gain respite from the baking sun. Physios, masseurs and athletes scrambled to grab the shaded areas like holiday-makers claiming poolside loungers with towels. The track was as unfinished as the accommodation with the land-scaping having been abandoned, trees and shrubs chaotically strewn about and there were four green, Glastonbury festival-esque green portaloos to accommodate athletes for when nature called. Even revelrous festival-goers would have turned their noses up at these humid, putrid toilets that weren't even worthy of Worthy Farm. In the past, this sort of stuff would have elicited complaining and moaning amongst the athletes, more accustomed to flying around in helicopters.

> "Stuff which would have bothered us in the past, maybe, if anything, pulled us closer together in Athens. We rolled our eyes at things that you could see other athletes wanting to complain about."
>
> — Darren Campbell

There had been so many bumps along the road since 1999, so many glaring examples of the bells and whistles not making a blind bit of difference to the performance of the team. Such inconveniences now barely brought about a shoulder shrug.

There were two warm up tracks in Athens, one slightly above the other. Britain were there very early and went for the higher track, looking down on the Americans. The Americans were surprised to turn up and find the British team occupying the higher ground and were even more surprised when there was no frivolity between them. They were accustomed to Darren in particular giving them some stick but partly because of his beef with Michael Johnson, partly down to the new team approach of focussing inwards, the British team blanked the Americans completely.

The USA team was number one and was as strong as any USA relay team in history with ridiculous firepower throughout. Even still, their coach John Smith was not looking very happy. Such things were conspicuous in an environment where every flinch, cough and look stood out, where rivals size each other up like teenagers at a disco. Small things were not going as he expected and he didn't like it.

The British team were operating on their own, impervious to any externalities while readying themselves for battle. They were relaxed and well-drilled, their personal coaches had let them be and handed over to Steve Perks. Everyone knew their roles. It felt as if it was going to be their night.

But they were ranked 15th in the world.

IT WAS QUIET, ON THE HIGHER TRACK, WARM IN THE SETTING SUN and to Mark it felt like something was hugging them. They did their warm up lap together, did their drills and skills and then began to rehearse passing the baton around. Britain's theme in their warm up was about projecting calmness and focussing on clean baton changes. The tip of the knife that is the very sharp end of sport walks a balance between simplicity and complexity that can sometimes confuse the mind. When each technique is broken down to the nth degree, when each stride is analysed for maximum optimisation, you can lose the wood for the trees. Having come through years of high-performance systems, of medals, titles and achievements, having learned through experiences at the highest possible level of elite sport, the team's pre-Olympic final strategy was no different to the one they would have encountered at their first ever relay race as juniors. The simple approach was for clean exchanges, to put the Americans under pressure as they had done in Paris a year previously and force them to make a mistake. They would expect Great Britain to wilt, to fall behind, to give up ground or even to make a catastrophic error. If they could just be a constant presence in the race, if they could refuse to go away, the USA might just make their own mistake. After a minimal amount of rehearsal, coach Steve Perks said, "That's enough." He knew they were ready.

Marlon was quietly confident. Having seen countless athletes borne on a tide of rising self-confidence have their dreams crushed, he had learned not to pay too much attention to pre-race appearances and shenanigans. Nevertheless, what he saw in his teammates' approach gave him great heart. Jason, Mark and Darren had not achieved their goals in their individual events and had been slated by the press. It could have been so easy for them to be disheartened but Marlon saw them smiling but determined, relaxed yet focussed. The team were unbothered by what was going on around them, projecting an aura of knowingness that must have bothered their opponents.

As the British team collected their things to leave the warmup track, picking up water bottles and various discarded items of clothing, they heard an uproar coming from the track below. It was the Americans. They were heading to the stadium full of exuberance and making a din, alerting all and sundry to their presence and to their apparent confidence. The British four slowly, quietly, collected their things and were the last team to head to the stadium. Remarkably, it was about a mile's walk away, a long distance for 100m sprinters! Mark was getting increasingly nervous as the stadium was approaching. The fizz from the arena was palpable, energy and electricity from the crowd reverberating out into the Greek night sky.

"You alright kid?" Darren asked him, sensing his nerves. Darren put his hand on Mark's shoulder and told him quietly, "We are going to win".

THEN STEVE PERKS STEPPED UP. HE'D PRESIDED OVER A RELAXED warmup, he'd seen the focus in his team, and now he wanted to give them a final shot of belief before they took on the world. As they approached the first call room for athlete registration, he encouraged them to seize the day. Having to translate "Carpe Diem" for Mark elicited some gentle laughter and eased a few nerves. As they walked through the belly of the stadium, Steve turned around and started to tell everyone how good they were, individually and as a collective. He demanded for them all to recognise that they were good enough to cope with what they'd find out on the track, that they were strong enough to deal with the pressures of the crowd and the occasion. He knew as well as they did that they had seen and felt the effects of pressure before. Now they were about to pile it onto others and see how they would deal with it.

As their coach, Perks was naturally heavily invested in the team's success. Success or failure would reflect on his abilities as well as the team's. He had shouldered this accountability to his superiors within UK Athletics since being appointed coach in 1998 and was humble enough to know that there had been many others who coveted his position. There were those who had questioned his appointment, not least because he would fulfil his commitments alongside his teaching job.

As a senior leader in education, Steve knew the propensity for bitterness and envy when it came to high level appointments and from day one, was aware that there were jealous, whispering voices in the background secretly waiting for him to fail. His wasn't a well-trodden path to elite coaching. He was from West Wales – hardly a hotbed of sprinting talent despite unearthing both Jamie Henthorn and Peter Maitland from there in the mid-1990s to compete at Commonwealth level – and everything from his accent to his demeanour was outside the norm for sprinting in the UK.

Steve Perks would ultimately end his career with Olympic, World and European Championship successes but he had a fire and a drive to prove himself as a top class coach. He burned for the success of the team and shared their desire to prove a few people wrong. This wasn't merely a professional commitment for Steve. He believed in the transformative power of sport and particularly in the stories of his athletes. He knew where they'd come from and while there were differences between them personally that he could never surmount, he certainly respected them.

> "I told them to imagine sitting in front of the fire with their grandchildren, telling them about their athletics careers and how their actions this one day would fill their lives with a memory that would never be beaten."
>
> — Steve Perks

He emphasised to the quartet the change that sport could create in people's lives before leaving for the track. They were living proof of where sport could take someone.

THE FINAL CALL AREA IN THE ATHENS STADIUM WAS A SMALL, featureless room. A lot of athletes lose themselves in this holding pen, faltering in the cramped air of machismo and naked aggression. Usually, people try to psych each other out and in Athens, many of the other teams were giving the British team their best heckles and putdowns rather than the Americans. It was either that the British resonated with a deep team spirit that everyone could see in that sweaty room or just that the other teams were afraid of being humiliated by the USA in ten minutes time and decided it was futile to rouse the favourites. Whatever their levels of arousal, they were on their own with no coaches allowed, thirty-two athletes ready for war.

After a while, the Americans joined in with the whooping, hollering and general boisterousness. It was like three dozen prize fighters about to walk into a Madison Square Garden heavyweight contest or a WWE Royal Rumble. The testosterone was flying but Jason, Darren, Marlon and Mark kept very quiet. They did not make eye contact with anyone except one other.

The uncharacteristic silence of the British team must have been disconcerting for the USA. The strong characters wearing the Union Jack would usually give as good as they got so this was unexpected. Perhaps the Americans, buoyed by their recent individual successes and after the debacle of the British semi-final performance, presumed that the GB team were already beaten.

Perhaps though, this approach from Great Britain did unsettle the USA. Back in 2001 at Edmonton, young John Barbour had been thrust into an unfamiliar situation with sights and sounds and senses flooding his brain, unused to anchoring a relay team at the highest level of competition. The USA team were now exposed to something very similar. They were used to the feeling and the emotions surrounding Olympic finals, a kaleidoscopic athletic experience where they were the stars, where they were centre stage. They were used to and relished being looked at. None of them had ever seen a team ignore them before. With their opponents not rising to their bait, the USA found themselves unsure. Were Great Britain aloof or afraid? The British team were solemn, but was this because they were full of nerves or full of focus? It was hard to tell.

This was like a warm up hit before a Wimbledon final with an opponent simply not hitting the balls back over the net. This was a presidential debate with one candidate simply nodding and not saying a word. Disconcerting. Unusual.

The call came from the officials. It was a long, low, concrete tunnel, dark and cold, from the holding room to the track. The athletes went from being a crew of prize-fighters awaiting their procession to gladiators being led to the baying masses through the underbelly of the coliseum. They were told by an official to put their bags down. Marlon paused and considered that the next time he would see his bag would be after the race. It felt strange to him, packing the winner's tracksuit that he might have to wear on the podium, leaving it behind for fate to decide. Every team, and every athlete, had subconsciously prepared for the eventuality of winning a medal, no matter how unlikely.

There were three calls for the athletes before entering the stadium. Like boarding a plane, some are eager and immediately bolt for position at the first opportunity while some hold back until the final call. The final call in athletics is when most teams head to the stadium, partly to project an aura of calmness and confidence. It sends the message to the others that, "We are the ones worth waiting for. Nobody is doing anything until we are there." Going on the first call traditionally signalled edginess, nerves and a degree of naivety. Experienced athletes would regard this entire process as a measure of a team's familiarity with high-level performance.

Great Britain entered at the first call. From having to qualify for the Games in the first place, not responding to the Americans' cat-calling, to their tranquil warmup, the entire preparatory process for the UK had gone against the grain. Why stop now?

This brought a few puzzled looks from their rivals and more bantering and baiting from the Americans but Britain were in their own psychological world, ready to command their own destiny. Britain spearheaded the walk into the stadium and in time, the rest of the field did the only thing they could do and followed suit. The rulebook wasn't being torn up, it was simply being left unopened.

For Jason, walking along the track to his starting blocks projected him back to his first school sports day. The Greek sun had baked the track all day long, the smell of burning rubber hanging in the air as it did when he was a boy back in Bath. He felt the tingle of anticipation that came with watching eyes, the focus on getting the best out of himself making him hyper-aware in the moment. He started to feel weak and empty and for a brief period, couldn't even put his leg forward due to the out-of-body weirdness of the occasion. He reverted to routine, checking all his equipment, his number, his blocks, his spikes; all the things that Dave Lease had taught him.

> "I always thought that when I was nervous or that my energy was being drained through anxiety, to simply control what I

> could. Check my equipment. Remind myself that I was in shape. Think of the opening few strides. Those things were within my power. In doing this I slowly started forgetting about the things I couldn't influence - and it was those things beyond my control that were the things usually making me nervous in the first place."
>
> — JASON GARDENER

Control the controllables. Do not take anything for granted. These feelings were no different in the Olympic final to when he was a schoolboy looking to prove himself to his peers in school. He'd been an outsider then and he was an outsider now. Only this time, he wasn't alone.

As he prepared his blocks, he exchanged a glance with the head official in the arena. Seeing this individual's face reminded Jason of a bizarre incident the day before, prior to the start of the semi-finals. The Greek official, completely unprompted, had told Jason, "You British are going to win."

Officials were not meant to interact with the athletes and this had stuck in Jason's mind. It now felt like another sign. The USA team was not being well received by the Greeks. Some of the Greek officials wanted their photos with the British athletes at first call rather than the Americans. Jason found this strange as on paper, the British team was nowhere near favourite to win. Darren had told the team to embrace it, that it was karma. The USA athletes were very surprised that the Greeks were making a fuss of the Brits and not of them.

As he walked around the bend to his start position on the back straight, Darren saw Jason settle on the start line. He felt extraordinarily confident. He completely ignored his American counterpart Justin Gatlin, not rising to any comment and avoiding any glare. Darren had the most reason of all to feel any doubt given that he had almost left the Games days before with a hamstring injury, but due to the faith and industry of his medical team and the belief and assurance of his team-mates, he was ready to test his health to the limit. He saw this as an opportunity to reach the greatest pinnacle in sport from the lowest depths of adversity. He had total conviction in his teammates to deliver, an unwavering, unearned belief that their best performance would win gold. Through ignoring him, choosing to interact on his own terms, Darren was going to unsettle Justin Gatlin as much before the race as he would during it. He knew these athletes as people. He knew what would make them pause for thought.

Darren's tranquillity could easily be misinterpreted. The confident Mancunian, normally the first to be in your face when a war of words ignited, was quiet, humourless and in his own world. Gatlin and his fellow athletes would have certainly been aware of the difficulties Darren had experienced the previous few days; exiting the individual events, murmurs of a torn hamstring, the spat with Michael Johnson. These factors, combined with an unusual quietness, suggested to teammates Gatlin and Coby Miller on the back straight that Campbell was out of the race mentally without it having even begun. Gatlin almost certainly mistook Campbell's concentration and confidence for meekness, timidity and a wish to hide.

Marlon had the long walk to the other side of the track. He concentrated on simply keeping warm, waiting for the whistle to warn the athletes that the race was merely minutes away. He told himself to focus on maximising his skillset and to keep calm. They had all learned that maintaining a buzz and keeping 'hyped' pre-race could counterintuitively lead to a draining of energy. He reminded himself that he was the best third leg sprinter in the world and that he was about to demonstrate this fact to millions. He felt confident and as he approached the far side of the bend, he looked over to Darren on the back straight, raised up his hand and gave a nod of approval, then turned and did the same to Mark who was pacing up and down the home straight. He placed his tape checkmark on the floor and emptied his mind except for one thought:

> 'As soon as Darren hits that mark, I'm gone.'

Mark was on the home straight. Through the hazy, swirling mirage of the heat, he could see the end of the track. When he got there, one team would have fulfilled their dreams and become Olympic Champions. His would be the longest wait. The youngest and the most inexperienced member of the team would have to deal with the most sledging, peacocking and bravado from the other teams. Not only that but two lanes over was the Kansas Cannonball Maurice Greene, double gold medallist from the Sydney Games and former world record holder for the 100m. Mark would need to show maturity beyond his years and composure beyond his experiences to fend Greene off, the kind of maturity and composure that the British press had been lambasting him for years for not having.

That night, Mark didn't mind all that. In fact, it gave him power. Jason, Darren, Marlon and Mark had dealt with tough upbringings, racism, classism, hardship and deprivation through strong personal choices, discipline, and composure. Exhibiting these traits on the track would merely be an extension of what they had experienced their entire lives. Getting the running right was the hard part, walking the high performance tightrope between glory and failure. For these four men, the peripheral stresses of the evening had become almost an irrelevance. They had experienced being let down by others, they'd learned from their own errors and had been taught the futility of arrogance both inside and outside of sport. Their tranquillity and solemnity in the face of the

Americans' taunting and the pressure of the occasion was not an act. For Mark, the gravity of the moment and its capacity to create an emotional drain was, this night under the Athens stars, met with minimal acknowledgment. Mark's persona on the track was aggressive, and he was certainly perceived as arrogant, but he felt that he had to step into character in order to go to war. Maurice Greene was never going to be able to snarl down someone from Smethwick. That leg, that night, at those Olympics, was somehow meant for Mark Lewis-Francis.

THE SHRILL WARNING WHISTLE REVERBERATED AROUND THE stadium. Jason picked up the baton, looking at it properly for the first time and smiled to himself. He realised it was gold in colour. Another sign. The stadium fell quiet as he was poised on his blocks. A deep hush. Moments later as the starter called them into the set position, he took a chance. He didn't usually jump guns, but he knew he needed to be at his absolute best. He also desperately wanted this Olympic medal. He went for it, jumped too early and immediately got called back. He jogged away as soon as the siren called the false start, seeing many others accelerate way into the distance. Walking back to the blocks, he knew it was him. There was no arguing the call and he maintained his calm.

Jumping had been a shot to nothing. If he'd got away on the gun then great. If not, he was the world 60m champion and fast starts were his specialty. The threat of disqualification now hung in the air and no one would think about trying to preempt the gun this time. He had piled the pressure on everyone else. Jason's goal for his leg was simply to take something out of the staggered start of a relay race. Shaun Crawford, who had won gold in the 200m days earlier was two lanes outside, and the objective was to close on everyone else while keeping Crawford on a leash. They settled back onto their blocks again, each athlete crouched, kicking their rear leg skywards before placing their spiked feet into the cushioned track base of the starting block.

Another cavernous hush descended on the stadium.

The gun crackled into the sky and Jason's second start was quite possibly better than his false first. Torso angling to the left, he surged into the bend. His spikes gripped the hot track, propelling him around the curve, his acceleration increasing with every stride. He ran aggressively, his legs whirring rapidly, his feet punching into the ground, expressing the power he had spent years cultivating on a hundred tracks and in countless weight rooms. With the gold baton in his right hand, held by his broken wrist, he maintained his speed while beautifully hugging the inside of the lane, careful not to touch the white line with his feet, an act which would have brought automatic disqualification. He closed in on the figure of Darren, who occupied the outside of his lane, driving low and hard away into the straight. Jason's speed endurance ensured there was plenty left in the tank as he came close to the end of his leg, propelling him forward and closing in rapidly on Darren. Years of practice playing the part with his team-mate and friend coupled with forensic analysis of their semi-final which had mostly reiterated the need for calmness of execution, brought Jason's outstretched 'push-pass' hand to meet Darren's long-armed palm in full flight.

The changeover was synchronised to perfection. The gold baton paused in mid-air horizontally, both athletes' hands outstretched, before it whipped back and forth piston-like in Darren's powerful arms as he accelerated away down the back straight. Jason chased after his team mate shouting encouragement as he slowed down, the Bath athlete having handed the responsibility of chasing gold to the Mancunian. Jason was now a nervous spectator with the other excited seventy-two thousand fans in the Spyros Louis Olympic Stadium, millions more watching the race unfold on live television across the world.

Darren powered away, his tall, straight posture a commanding presence on the back straight. He was focused on chasing down Justin Gatlin, two lanes to his right, while also keeping his eyes fixed on the figure of Marlon Devonish astride his lane some ninety metres away. He was in full flight by the time Jason had handed him the baton, the changeover not hampered by even a half stride, the two of them exhibiting a perfect fluidity. Campbell – undeterred by the very real prospect of tearing a hamstring in an Olympic final – hammered down on every stride as if it was his last, bringing all his power to bear on the gap between him and Gatlin. He'd shut off all of his peripheral senses as he closed in on Marlon waiting to receive the baton. All he decided to see would be the rapidly approaching Marlon in his lane, all he heard the staccato sound of his sixteen spikes fluttering on the track accompanying the heavy breathing of his rivals. Everything else was blank.

Coach Steve Perks was sat in the stand at the 200m start mark, where Darren would soon be transferring the baton to Marlon. While he was now just another thrilled spectator unable to influence proceedings, his coaching eye was still attuned. He had a similar view of the race as the outgoing third leg runners. He noticed the spike plate underneath the huge feet of Darren Campbell glistening in the reflected light of the stadium, coming towards him like a freight train. Darren's high knee lift, his physical presence in his lane and the flashes of bright, white, reflected light from under his spikes drew the eye, even from his position in the stands. Perks also knew that in the tripod position that most athletes held while waiting for their teammates to reach them before transferring the baton, the low head position, the curvature of the bend and the rotated posture of the body in that stance made it almost impossible to see the incoming runner from your own team. You would see only that of the team outside. The only thing that Coby Miller from the USA would have presumably been able to see were Marlon's feet two lanes inside him and this highly distracting sight of Campbell's aggressively pumping, flashing strides.

Marlon was looking at Darren coming towards him. Arms flexed powerfully, eyes flickering, Darren was running for his life. As soon as he approached the taped checkmark on the track which signified the time for Marlon to accelerate away, Devonish averted his gaze to look at nothing but Campbell's feet and his tape. He went into the three-point crouched position and as soon as Darren's feet hit the mark, Marlon drove away explosively in order to get up to speed. Through the mess of colliding hands and bodies, he could sense Darren closing in on him, even as he sprinted at maximum speed in the opposite direction. He heard Darren shout "hand" and with his arm outstretched behind him, he felt the slap of the baton fill his palm and with it, adrenaline tore through his body like a bursting dam. Marlon let rip. All his pre-race frustrations about not getting to run in the 200m all came out in anger. The baton smashing into his hand released him and Marlon turned on the emotional afterburners that he had been withholding deep inside. His eyes widened, internally he shouted "it's...my...turn!!!" and with that came the elation and freedom of running.

Each stride between the two British athletes was synchronised to perfection. The 0.8 second window to exchange the baton, even when travelling at 25mph, seemed like an eternity to execute the skill that they had perfected between them over the years and throughout their careers. It felt so easy. Marlon sped around the bend. He was aware of something having happened behind him and outside him during the changeover but was focused on chasing down the Nigerian team in the lane outside. Coby Miller, the American, was obstructed from Marlon's view by Nigeria's Aaron Egbele. This meant that the stagger had been closed on the Americans. Marlon chased hard and closed on Egbele as the inside curve also ate up the stagger. As he approached the relay box, he fixed his gaze beyond Mark – not to where he was currently standing, but to where they would be exchanging the baton. With thirty metres to go, in full stride at full speed, Marlon focused on the imposing physique of Mark Lewis-Francis and readied himself for the most important two seconds of his life.

THREE MINUTES EARLIER, MARK LEWIS-FRANCIS WAS STANDING relaxed at the top of the home straight of the Olympic Stadium, collecting his thoughts and watching keenly as team-mate Jason Gardener got down on to his blocks for the start. The stadium was silent except for the bleats of a few rowdy fans, keen for their voices to be heard at the start of an Olympic final. He could see Maurice Greene, three metres to his right, pacing menacingly up and down the relay box, imposing his presence on the competition. The bravado and swagger amongst all the athletes which had dominated the previous five minutes dissipated, the anchor leg runners let their masks fall away as they settled to focus and to perform. There had been a false start and from his viewpoint a hundred metres away, Mark thought it might have been Jason. He told himself not to worry and to continue to focus. Others around him had slapped their thighs in frustration and let out a couple of exasperated gasps but he was calm. Calmer than he should have been. He was twenty-one years of age and about to bring the British team home in an Olympic final against some of the world's best ever athletes.

Then silence descended on the arena once more.

His shoulders flinched with excitement at the crack of the gun and at seeing Jason get out so well. The race was on. The roar from the crowd drowned out everything else and he could feel his heart racing with adrenaline. He once again looked at his checkmark on the track behind him, and took a few deep breaths. With the race in full flow, he could see the smooth transition between Jason and Darren and once the tall figure of Campbell took flight down the back straight, Mark tried to place himself in Darren's position, instinctively trying to feel out the race that was rapidly closing in on him. Once again, he looked at the checkmark. He settled. At this point there was silence. He was deep within the cocoon of his own concentration. He could no longer hear the crowd's deafening roar. All he could hear was breathing. There was the occasional nervous jitter of his competitors' spikes as they prepared themselves but nothing more. As Marlon came around the bend like a steam train, Mark once again stared at the checkmark, waited what seemed like an eon for Marlon's feet to appear and with his cheeks puffing and blowing, drove out as hard as he was physically able.

He then felt the baton slap into his left hand.

> "I remember coming off the bend and thinking, 'Wow. I'm in first place.' From that moment, everything went blank."
>
> — Mark Lewis Francis

Fresh from his starting leg, Jason jogged back around the bend opposite to the finish line, breathing hard after his exertions, watching Marlon tear around the final bend. There had been a commotion on the second changeover and despite it being unclear who was involved, it looked like the Nigerians were very much ahead and having a particularly good race. Darren had looked phenomenal on his leg and from Jason's vantage point, it seemed Marlon was making a real impression on the medal placings. His senses heightened at the prospect of seeing the entire field haring down the home straight and for a moment he froze with doubt. With Britain, Nigeria and America ahead of the field, it looked a little like anchor leg runner Mark had left slightly early for the baton handover from Marlon. Thankfully, he realised his fears were misplaced. Mark and Marlon exchanged in first and Lewis-Francis was powering down the home straight towards him, delivering his dreams.

Darren had exchanged his baton with Marlon and having decelerated slowly to protect his hamstring collapsed on the far side of the track by the 200m start. On his hands and knees, he rested his forehead on the hot Athens track and attempting to block out the emotional carnage raging all around, closed his eyes and whispered a prayer to himself. He had done what he had promised his teammates and coaches and fulfilled what he had promised himself days earlier.

Seconds later, Marlon was at the top of the home straight seeing Mark Lewis-Francis sprint away from him in first place. For a split second, there had been a feeling that he was not going to reach him and at that point he shouted "hand" and slapped the baton into Mark's hand. As soon as the baton was released, Marlon felt Mark surge away and he shouted "GOOOO". Then, he felt the same surge come from Maurice Greene. By the time he had the chance to look and take stock of the situation, he realised that the Americans had exchanged the baton after the British team. He jogged down the home straight, half slowing down and half striding, to urge his friend on to glory. He glanced up at the stadium screen and could see Mark ahead, with Maurice Greene chasing him. With about thirty metres to go, Mark pulled away from the Nigerian Deji Aliu and a wave of realisation hit Marlon that he was in the home straight of the Olympic track, in front of Greece's biggest television witnessing Mark, forty metres away from him, chasing gold. Yet even in the excitement of the moment, Marlon found it impossible not to briefly think about the year before in Paris when Dwain had been caught by J.J. Johnson.

This time it felt different.

> "I want to say, around five metres from the finish line, I think I heard Maurice Greene.
>
> I dipped as I crossed the line, and with my head turned I exploded in emotion thinking:
>
> 'I got him'."
>
> — Mark Lewis-Francis

Marlon had his hands in the air. As soon as he saw Mark cross the line, he was almost certain they had won. Still, he wasn't sure; the team had become accustomed to things not going their way and a defence mechanism was already in action, readying Marlon to accept the fact that something would go against them. When the confirmation of victory came from the scoreboard, the crescendo of emotion hit him full force. The boy who walked home from Kirby Corner athletics track in Coventry listening to his own mixtapes, jogged the last twenty metres of the home straight of the Athens Stadium to the sound of a crowd celebrating him as Olympic Champion.

Jason just knew they'd won. He found himself among the throng of athletes and officials near the start line. He had always heard about the feeling of being 'in the zone' psychologically and at this moment he was deep in his. The race he had just witnessed merely confirmed and validated the confidence and feeling he had experienced that entire day. He gasped at the realisation of his achievement.

Meanwhile at the end of the back straight, Darren was interrupted by the gallant gentleman Uchenna Emedolu of Nigeria. Emedolu knelt down to tap Darren on the shoulder, almost apologetically interrupting his prayer, to tell him:

> "Darren, you're Olympic Champion."

16

> "Everything you've dreamt of your whole life, everything you've wanted to achieve, everything you've worked hard for, all the suffering, all the pain, all the injuries, all that.... irrelevant.
>
> You've just got an Olympic Gold Medal."
>
> — Mark Lewis-Francis

They had been in a state of deepest concentration. Arranged around the Athens track, each of them alone but together, connected by a trained and harnessed intuition. All distractions in the arena blocked out. A focus on the moment so profound that nothing else existed.

Thirty-eight seconds later.

Mark's scream of exhilaration when crossing the line brought them all out from their emotional bubbles. Leaping around, he roared to the heavens, knowing that this victory would, in future, give his family something to be proud of.

Marlon had handed the baton to Mark and not stopped running, chasing him down the home straight. As he ran he looked up, watching the climax of the race on the massive screen. He saw the biggest moment of his life unfold on tv, like everyone else around the world, before joining Mark at the finish line and embracing him.

Jason felt uncontrollably alive, coursing with emotion. He felt an overwhelming need to be with his team and he ran and crashed into Mark and Marlon in a collision of pure elation.

The enormity of the moment had hit Darren hard. He was walking slowly around the bend to the home straight and he could not stop crying. All the tears he'd never cried, that he'd suppressed his whole life, all came out in floods of happiness. He knew this was his last race in his last Olympic Games and his euphoria was not just from crowning his sporting career, but from overcoming almost thirty years of hardship and adversity. His mind was awash with so many memories and feelings, of being back on the estate, of people who'd come in and out of his life, of dreams dashed and realised.

THEY HAD VISUALISED THE ACT OF WINNING OLYMPIC GOLD A thousand times. Since childhood, they'd dreamed of how it would feel to be standing on the rostrum, bowing to receive the medal. No matter what they'd imagined, they weren't ready for the emotions they encountered on their lap of honour. They'd entered a dream-like haze, asking 'Is this really, truly, happening?", while being assailed by a breath-taking visual and sonic extravaganza that assured them it was. What seemed like a thousand Union Jacks appeared on the bleachers. From blocking out all the noise, focussed on nothing but the task, they could suddenly hear every single voice in the crowd calling their names. It felt like the entire stadium was on their side. They went over to pockets of the crowd where they had photos with fans and with fellow British athletes. On the track there were people who had been involved in their careers for years, who had seen them grow and now had seen them become champions. Photographer Mark Shearman had been a mainstay of British athletics for decades whose smile and good wishes they had all appreciated from their junior days all the way to now. With the world's media becoming frantic in capturing 'the' celebration photo with their big lenses, they all wanted to give Mark the best shot. They also saw the by-now-notorious Greek track judge that had predicted their victory to Jason, and thanked him for his mystic prowess.

The athletics media were delighted by their success. These were people who had a duty to compliment and to criticise according to performances but now that they were beaming and sharing in the glory, the team realised that the press really had wanted them to win. There was earnest human integrity here, a solidarity that they'd not often felt. The lap of honour bought them precious moments to return down to earth.

They held hands aloft as they mounted the podium, taking their place at the top. The Americans were very graceful in defeat. Maurice Greene and Coby Miller, despite their personal disappointments, showed refinement and dignity in their sincere congratulations. Atop the podium, Jason and Darren pinched each other on the rostrum before the medal presentation, one final confirmation that this was real, Jason pushing his nail into his thumb to make sure he really wasn't dreaming.

Athletics is a tough sport. Rare moments of glory can come your way but that glory is very individual indeed. To share such a feeling with three teammates, to have others there to understand, crowned their journey from rivals to brothers.

With wreaths on their heads, gold medals tight against their chests, the drum roll started and the crowd fell silent. The Union flag rose higher than the USA and Nigerian flags as God Save The Queen filled the Spyros Louis Olympic Stadium. They stood as a four in the same order as they had run. Mark surrendered to the moment, his eyes misty, content and happy. Marlon could not stop smiling. He kept glancing to the heavens, a suggestion of a head shake hinting at his disbelief. Darren was emotionally charged. Head bowed, face contorted with teary joy, feeling the gravity of the moment. Jason simply stared at the flag, unflinching, steely and proud.

---

4 HOURS LATER

DARREN WAS ON THE BRANDIES WHEN THE OTHERS CAUGHT UP with him. The night out in Athens saw them surfing on a sea of expensive liquor and champagne. Jason was in bed, exhausted from recovering from major surgery, experiencing the birth of his first child and winning Olympic Glory in a matter of months. Out on the town, the club owners and the public treated Mark, Darren and Marlon like royalty. Outside the pubs and bars, burly Greek security guards pushed them to the front of every line, handing out bottles and shouting to those on the streets, "These guys beat the Americans!" The boys from Manchester, Coventry and Smethwick had the freedom of Greece, being celebrated at every turn.

As the night wore on, the mayhem let up for a moment and in that minute's peace, they came to realise what they had achieved. One moment stuck with Marlon; the three of them, drinks in hand, sharing a silence outside a nightclub on the beach, taking it all in as they watched the lights shine over the Aegean Sea. After all the exuberance and the revelry within the stadium, the emotion of the medal presentation, the carnival atmosphere of being embraced as heroes on the streets, what really brought it home was this stillness, silence and serenity, listening to the waves lapping against the shore.

The following morning they were all absolutely hanging. Being highly tuned athletes coming off the back of months of asceticism, their alcohol tolerance was at a lifetime low while their consumption the previous night had been at an all-time high. Even glittering gold medals could not alleviate their pounding headaches. They went back to the village for a 9am press conference, showering in ice cold water, slapping their cheeks and gulping down any liquid they could get their hands on. Marlon almost missed the press conference altogether while Darren just managed to dress himself properly in his GB tracksuit. Fortunately they could rely on Jason to face the media, fresh from a good night's sleep.

Later in the day, after Darren became possibly the first gang member from Sale Racecourse to eat crab with the British Ambassador to Greece at the Embassy, they all decided to go and watch some sport. They had not done this once during the Olympic Games. They had gone to Athens to do their jobs. The best athletes always had a cold, ruthless approach to the spectacle of the Olympics, refusing to lose their edge and give in to bright lights and distractions. During the pre-Olympic camp in Paphos, they had met a likeable teenage boxer by the name of Amir Khan and decided to go and support him in his final bout where he won a silver medal.

After the euphoria of the previous day, the thought of returning home was a tantalising one. Gold medal winners flew business class. More leg room, better meals and a choice of films were the reward for achieving your life's ambition. Upon arrival at Heathrow, the medal winners got paraded into the arrivals hall in front of hundreds of people. As soon as they won, their lives ceased to be their own. There were countless press conferences. They turned on the Christmas lights in London with the actors from the Harry Potter series. They got letters notifying them of receiving MBEs, as well as honorary Greek citizenships and the freedom of the city of Athens. Marlon, Mark and Jason met the Queen at Buckingham Palace in a reception, wondering all the while, "How had council estate kids, state school strugglers, ended up here?"

While all this was good fun, Darren, Jason and Mark all had young children to return to. Life had become slightly surreal and they wanted normality for a few days. Jason just wanted to see his wife Nancy and daughter Molly. Darren didn't have a party upon returning to Manchester. He simply wanted quiet time with his family and to show his medal to his friends. By the time Marlon had returned home to Coventry, the BBC had already been to the Devonish household and the family had quiet drinks at home to celebrate. Everyone was desperate to see the medal. When he told his mum that he had been awarded an MBE, she started laughing and crying all at once, bursting with joy and pride.

Mark was still overwhelmed by the idea of being Olympic champion. The phone at the family home had been blowing up for days with people sending their congratulations. He thought doors would open from that moment on but as all four of them were about to discover, they would be surprised.

THE BBC SPORTS PERSONALITY OF THE YEAR AWARDS IS AN unmissable part of the sporting calendar for the British sports fan. The judging panel for Team of the Year consisted of 30 sports experts drawn from a selection of newspaper sports editors, representatives from the BBC and individuals from sports governance and broadcasting. At the time, the sports involved in the team award tended to reflect a certain demographic of society: cricket, rowing, rugby, golf. The term 'team' was a fluid one; ice skaters Torvill and Dean had won the 'team' award in 1982 and 1983, then winning the 'individual' award in 1984 after their Sarajevo Olympic triumph. The previous Olympic year in 2000, the entire Olympic and Paralympic teams were chosen as team winners. A team could be a team of two or two thousand.

Track and field athletics was almost universally merit-based. The quickest, farthest and highest won. Jason, Darren, Marlon and Mark had all succeeded or failed according to their performance levels during their careers. There was no room for subjectivity. While the committee of experts had crowned many deserving winners in the past, the system was open to subjectivity, unlike track and field.

As the envelope was opened on stage, the coxless fours rowing team were anointed Team of the Year; a deserving victory celebrating a consistency of performance from the medal machine that was British Rowing. This argument could also be made for the British Sailing team which in 2004 was on its second phase of winning gold in three consecutive Olympic Games. For whatever reason, a foreseeable victory in rowing eclipsed the startling victory on the track.

Almost two decades later, the relay team triumph of Athens 2004 would still be considered one of the most unexpected and surprising shocks in modern sport. Like Team of the Year award winners Leicester City winning the Premier League in 2016, this was one of the biggest upsets in sporting history but while Leicester won with 2 games still to play, the relay team won gold by 0.01 of a second.

Was this a fluke? Was this a lucky victory by the smallest of margins or was this something that had been planned, prepared for and executed? Did Shaun Crawford, Maurice Greene, Coby Miller and Justin Gatlin enjoy their successes a little too much after the individual events? Did they lose a bit of their edge, having run multiple races in both the 100m and the 200m events? The USA should by right, have won gold by near-on nine metres considering their cumulative times over 100m. This was, after all, the best-ever USA sprint relay team and even in 2021, prevailing wisdom is that 'if you are hiring a sprint relay team, you select the fastest runners.'[1]

But that's not how relays work. You don't just throw the fastest athletes together and expect it to add up to success. The British team had learned that through bitter experience. This was a triumph of planning, practice and performance, of sporting synergy coming together to deliver on the biggest stage when it mattered most. 0.01 of a second suggests that there was no space for anything but perfection from the GB team. There was no other team within range of the Americans to challenge for gold. The Brits, like they had done in Paris the previous year and in Seville in 1999, had breathed down the Americans' necks. This time, the Americans had flinched.

Is winning on the line lucky? Was Michael Jordan's legendary last-second shot from deep in 1998 to sink the Utah Jazz lucky? Is South Africa's 2007 Rugby World Cup triumph lucky because Mark Cueto's try in the corner was disallowed? The beauty of sport is that the most miniscule variable can affect the script, that the flap of a butterfly's wing can cause a tornado. In the biggest moments, small margins create champions.

Perhaps this was "only a relay medal"? Champions of that opinion would have to, for consistency's sake, also hold the achievements of some of Britain's most celebrated Olympians, including Steve Redgrave, Geraint Thomas, Katherine Grainger and Matthew Pinsent under the same auspices. Most of their medals were achieved as part of a team. In the final medals tally at the Olympic Games, no nation is questioning where each gold medal comes from in their hunger to top the table. A gold is a gold.

In 2015, Jason Gardener became the president of UK Athletics. In his dealing with high level organisations in the UK and elsewhere, more often than not he would be the only non-white person in the room. He still stands out, as he did at school in Bath in the 1980s. Well into the twenty-first century, if you are a chief executive you are probably a white male.

Which is ironic because within sprinting, certainly during his career timespan, a lazy perception existed that you were successful because you were black. There remains an insinuation between the success of black sprinters and the notion that their success is purely rooted in being genetically gifted. Almost as if Jason, Darren, Marlon and Mark were destined to be quick, never mind their years of dedication, mastering the technicalities of one of the most pressurised events there is, the late night bus rides or long walks home, the missed social occasions and countless gruelling training sessions.

Contrast this with rowing, or cycling in its team or individual incarnations. The perception is of 5am starts, tortuous efforts for hours on end in inhospitable environments, of the winners being the ones with the strongest work ethic or the most elevated pain thresholds. There is no room for luck, gift, or fortune in the equation when it comes to these sports. Steve Redgrave, Chris Hoy, Geraint Thomas and Victoria Pendleton are the most 'dedicated' and 'hard-working' beneficiaries of a 'culture of marginal gains' and 'quests for perfection'. There's a narrative, even among sports people themselves, constantly reinforcing this gap between a 'gift' bestowed on an unwitting individual who suddenly finds themselves with phenomenal athletic abilities without having to do much and an individual's chosen dream, cultivated through years of toil, sweat, tears and sacrifice. Rowers and cyclists put themselves through rigorous regimens and optimise to perfection. Sprinters just turn up and run fast.

A Formula One pitstop is known for being one of the most jaw-dropping feats of communication and coordination in sport. Tyres and wheels changed, cars refuelled and back racing in five seconds. It showcases the finest mechanics and engineers demonstrating their incredible technique, dexterity and skill, operating under phenomenal pressure where microseconds count. It's celebrated and fetishised as an example of superb teamwork and a model for high performance environments.

The relay handover is a Formula One pitstop.

This 0.8 seconds whirr of hands and feet, this transferring of an object at the limits of human performance, performed in a confined space within the tiniest of windows only receives scrutiny when done badly and not when it is done well. When it came to the post-event celebration of their achievement of winning gold, there is no doubt that even on a subconscious level, the four athletes fought against the trope of genetic gifts, the perception of the event and their good fortune at others' mistakes. It served to immediately devalue their achievement in the narrative of British sport.

Jason, Darren, Marlon, Mark, Steve Perks, Graham Knight, Christian Malcolm, Nick Smith, Chris Lambert, Dwayne Grant and Aki Salo all came together as a team determined to align themselves to a singular goal, whether they would be on the podium at the end or not. This was a beautiful concept, years in the making. They believed in a collective mission. Their respective personalities and life experiences helped them prevail. Their confidence came from the faith they had in one another.

The coaches, consciously or not, had aligned the personalities of the athletes to the strategies required in the race. First leg, Jason – a fast starter with a devastatingly accurate changeover that could handle pressure. Second leg, Darren - a headstrong inner-city boy with a point to prove, an 'eat-or-be-eaten' attitude combined with an appetite to run people down. Third leg, Marlon – professional and reliable but radiating hunger and running like a man possessed. Fourth leg, Mark – aggressive, fearless and someone who would be running fuelled by anger as much as adrenaline. Their skill sets met the demands of the occasion.

Even logistical coincidences were embraced and adapted to. Marlon and Mark hadn't qualified for the latter stages at Athens so they trained, and trained some more, on their baton exchanges. It clicked in the final, the pair making the necessary adjustments from the faltering semi-final to bring it home. There were also the signs – the gold baton, the officials saying they wanted them to win, the Americans and Nigerians trying to psych everyone out and quite possibly draining themselves in the process. It felt like everything that happened was supposed to happen. Four people believed in the same thing and there was never any doubt. Even the false start felt like it was part of the plan.

The plan had worked. The team had gone from 15th in the world to Olympic gold within a year but did anyone learn from this success? Future quartets 'lurched from one failure to the next'[2] and, with the exception of a World Championship bronze in 2009, endured a litany of dropped batons and disqualifications until a surprise World Championship gold in London in 2017. Athens 2004 was a blueprint on how to win a relay race, on how to deconstruct an event and optimise for its demands, on how to face down and defeat a seemingly superior foe, wasted due to thinking it was a flukey one-off.

This attitude looks like even more of an oversight when contrasted with the attitude towards winners in the USA. The lucrative and prestigious NCAA collegiate system is full of ex-athletes in highly paid coaching or program coordinator roles, supported by well-funded systems of recruitment and resources specifically designed to enhance their chances of success. American sprint legends Carl Lewis and Leroy Burrell run the University of Houston's track programme. Carmelita Jeter joined the University of Alabama's backroom team. Maurice Greene was hired by UCLA. Talent from the highest peak of the sport was immediately reinvested into the developmental system. Maybe this wasn't anything to do with philosophy, sports governance or indeed skin colour. Maybe it was simply a national difference in attitude.

The American celebration of black excellence extended beyond the athletics track. In the cut-throat world of entertainment where the dollar often speaks louder than politics, Americans were becoming accustomed to seeing black accomplishments celebrated on their own merit. As early as the 1980s, America promoted, valued, commercialised and sold their black talent to the world. Then as now in American culture, if people thought you were good enough, the USA propelled you onto the world stage with commercial gusto as emblematic of American exceptionalism. Michael Jordan, Prince, Michael Jackson, Oprah Winfrey, Denzel Washington, Whitney Houston, Will Smith and Stevie Wonder. Not only culturally but commercially significant.

There can be no doubt that despite this veneer of equality on the grand scale, racism was and still is prevalent within American society. The successes of black people in American public life belied the struggle that most suffered, with the vast majority of African Americans more often than not found at the lower end of the socioeconomic scale.

Nevertheless, black American culture was American culture. They were one and the same. Black people were a ubiquitous part of American stardom, be that the arts, music, television, movies or sport.

Considering the legacy and history of American sport within this context, the long line of megastar names within individual sports extended to the Athens Olympic Games. The American teams in the Olympiads immediately before and after Athens 2004 were stacked full of bonafide sporting deities. Shaquille O'Neal, Michael Phelps, Carl Lewis, Michael Johnson, Allyson Felix, Mia Hamm, Andre Agassi, Floyd Mayweather Jr, Jennifer Capriati, Michael Jordan, Oscar De La Hoya, Venus Williams, Serena Williams, Hope Solo, Kobe Bryant, LeBron James. These globally significant names had a level of fame, commercial value and celebrity status that transcended their sport. Half of the American Men's 4x100m team that Britain defeated, namely Maurice Greene and Justin Gatlin, also belonged in this rarefied company. These weren't just huge sports stars. They were huge names and they were black athletes.

With this wildly unexpected victory, Jason, Darren, Marlon and Mark had overcome American sporting exceptionalism and national expectation by defeating them at one of their most prized endeavours; having the quickest men on the planet. This achievement didn't necessitate television deals or faces on cereal boxes but it did expose a key difference between the two nations, namely - where was the celebration of black British success?

Where was the British Prince? Whitney? Spike Lee? Oprah?

Where was the British Michael Jordan? Carl Lewis? Williams sisters?

Where were the black musicians, artists, presenters or sportspeople celebrated with profile and pride, financially compensated in line with their achievements and held up alongside the Union Jack as symbols of national identity?

Linford Christie had defeated Carl Lewis on multiple occasions, but to compare the esteem in which Lewis was held in the USA to the position Christie held in the British psyche was laughable. The only Black Briton truly on the world stage at the time was supermodel Naomi Campbell who was often castigated for her behaviour, while Frank Bruno became world boxing champion but was fast-tracked into pantomime. Even Lennox Lewis who became undisputed heavyweight champion of the world defeating the likes of Mike Tyson, Evander Holyfield and Vitali Klitschko, struggled to have his achievements recognised at the time in Britain and his legacy only achieved its proper status through the lens of history. John Barnes was arguably one of the most talented football players in the world but despite appearing in a Lucozade Sport advert and an iconic-in-retrospect spoken interlude in New Order's World Cup single, he remained outside of the megastar category in Britain. Lenny Henry was as celebrated and respected for openly criticising the lack of diversity of talent in British television as he was being a talent on television itself.

British culture during this period was bright white. The profile, remuneration and cultural significance given to Premiership football stars was yet to reach today's heights and the days of embracing Lewis Hamilton, Stormzy and Dina Asher-Smith as 'one of our own' were still a decade away. In beating iconic sprinters from across the pond at their own game, Britain had fired a shot across the bow of the American cultural armada but there was no doubt in 2004 which side of the Atlantic celebrated winners irrespective of their skin colour.

Celebrations aside, British gold medals at Athens 2004 proved crucial for the road to the London Olympics in 2012. Had

Kelly Holmes not won her gold an hour before the relay and had Jason, Darren, Marlon and Mark had not won theirs, British Athletics would have lost millions of pounds from the next funding cycle for Beijing. The newspapers were correct in their assessment that there was a price attached to each medal and that the black holes in the governing body's spreadsheets that needed filling with funding got deeper and darker in the absence of any golden glint. These two golds right at the end of the Athens Games not only saved the blushes of the British athletics establishment but also ensured a continuity of funding, resources and coaching positions. Sighs of relief would have been heard along the corridors of power as Mark's vest crossed the line a fraction of a centimetre before Maurice Greene's chest. Along with Dame Kelly's golds and Kelly Sotherton's Heptathlon bronze, the relay gold allowed the status quo to be extended and justified for at least one more Olympic go around. It enabled a narrative of 'building towards the next cycle' to continue which would have had zero mandate had the Athens Olympics been a medal-less blowout for the British Team. Without black athletes delivering in Athens, the GB triumphs of Beijing might have played out somewhat differently.

Yet unlike the American athletes who would have received upwards of $50,000 for being Olympic Champions, or the Greeks who were incentivised and rewarded to the tune of a reported €150,000 to become home Olympic winners, the British team were given a hearty well done and whatever bonuses they could negotiate from their personal sponsors. The money their successes generated flowed straight back to their respective governing bodies leading on to the next Olympic cycle.

Winning Olympic Gold meant navigating a perilous, challenging path to get to the top of the mountain, but the team found that on the other side of the highest peak of sporting achievement lay a steep cliff and a deep chasm. The anticipated financial rewards did not come. The plaudits and awards from peers did not come. A level of respect usually bestowed upon Olympic champions was found to be conspicuously absent. They had returned home to momentary fame and celebration but they returned to the same houses, with the same precarious job prospects as other athletes, without any of the trappings of wealth or success that football, rugby, snooker, tennis, or golf players would enjoy in winning the major at Augusta, or the World Cup, or Wimbledon. They had achieved their life's goal, and at the same time as dealing with the anti-climatic emptiness of the question, "So what happens now?" they had to reconcile their perceived status with their financial realities. Wives, children, parents and friends celebrated their win, full in the knowledge that they had also sacrificed their time and energies for the team to pursue the highest accolade in sport. They all believed that their lives would change at that moment, that the years of selfless sacrifice would lead to a smoother path and a better outlook in life. To find that this wasn't the case felt like a betrayal.

THAT NIGHT IN ATHENS

THAT NIGHT IN ATHENS, JASON, DARREN, MARLON AND MARK knew that whatever came next, their lives would no longer be the same. Life was now divided into before and after winning Olympic Gold. While they had all dreamed of individual glory, getting to share sporting immortality was a surprising gift, one that would stay with them forever. Where they had once been alone, they were now united. Where they were once rivals, now they were teammates. Where once they were outsiders, now they were champions.

Whatever was to follow they would be forever entwined, experiencing eternity in that moment, a feeling that only they could know on that night in Athens when they came together and shocked the world in 38.07 seconds.

While others might remember the photo finish or the smiles and tears on the rostrum, the moment that they remember was a different one, one between achievement and recognition, between the deed and the reward, shared just by them out there on the track.

In that one moment they found each other, joined together and embraced one another, dropped to one knee and said a prayer of thanks.

They enjoyed a special moment connected to one another, joyous and grateful, still in a sea of spectacle. A moment imprinted in time, a moment to tell their grandchildren about, kneeling united in the arena in a photograph to be cherished forever.

This team never raced again.

ACKNOWLEDGMENTS

Firstly, it's impossible to name everyone individually who contributed to our journey to Athens. Those who played a part know who they are and we'd like to thank you all. Nevertheless we do have some individuals to thank both for supporting us on the track and in the creation of this book.

It would be remiss for us to not thank Nick Smith, Dwaine Grant, Chris Lambert and Christian Malcolm. As part of the relay squad, they gave themselves wholly to the team and played their parts to the very best of their ability despite ultimately knowing they were not going to be on the starting line in Athens.

We also want to thank every person that has been part of relay teams in the past, whether as an athlete or as part of the support staff. Results aside, it was the lessons learnt along the way that refined our planning and laid the foundations for our success in Athens.

We have to give a sincere thanks to the British public for playing the National Lottery! Without the lottery, funding would not have been provided to elite sport and we would not have been able to prepare as we did. Our personal sponsors down the years also deserve a mention in this respect.

Most importantly, the volunteers, teachers, parents, coaches up and down the country who make athletics work and provide accessible opportunities to people like us who get to live a life beyond our wildest dreams and expectations.

Thanks to Larry Achike OLY, Adidas, Malcolm Arnold, Mark Avis, Anthony Barrett, Sue Barrett, Baskervilles Gym, Bath Sports Centre, Beechen Cliff School, Stefania Bello, Tim Benjamin OLY, Alun & Jill Bevan, Bisham Abbey High Performance Centre, Neil Black, Roger Black OLY, Mark Brodie, Andy Burke, Ian Byers, Caludon Castle School, Aaryn Campbell, Clair Campbell, Dillan Campbell, Leoni Campbell, Marva Campbell, Robin Chakraverty, Kate Channon, Darren Chin, Linford Christie, Matt Church, City of Bath AC (particularly Diane) Pete Clarke, Steve Clarke, Paula Clayton, Jenny Close, all at Clickbox, Sarah Connors, Jane Cowmeadow, Angela Cullen, Culverhay School, Justin Daniels, Rhodri Davies, Anthony Devonish, Cheryl Devonish, Desmond Devonish, Errol Devonish, Vivian Devonish, Paul Dijksta, Dan Donovan, Srdjan Dragutinovic, Bryan English, Ayo Falola, Fila, Karben Forbes, Zara Ford, George Gandy, Catherine Gardener, Carl Gardener, Jessica Gardener, Nancy Gardener, Brendon Ghent, Andrew Gill, Wayne Girdleston, Mark Green, John Headley, Mark Hylton OLY, King Edward's School Bath, Sir Eddie Kulukundis, Sarah Jones, Dave Lease, Tony Lester, Sophia Livert, Jonathan Marks, Chris Martin, Paul Martin, Tracey Martin, the Mees, Kim Mercer, Moorlands School, Wayne Morant, Kay Murphy, James McIlroy OLY, Simon Nathan, Abi Oyepitan OLY, Pace Sports Management, Annie Payne, Pedro Philippou, the Ron Pickering Memorial Fund, Steve Platt, Noel Pollock, Matt Press, Puma, John Regis, Marcia Bailey OLY, Mark Richardson OLY, Lowri Roberts, Dafydd Roberts, Peter Roscoe, Alison Rose, Nicole

Sanders OLY, Ricky Simms, Matt Shirvington OLY, St. John's School, Jennifer Stoute, Mark Sinclair, Samantha Stear, Jenny Sullivan, the Swabys, test readers James, Ben, Matt and Derek, Thames Valley Athletic Centre, University of Bath, Martin Waldron, Ashleigh Wallace, Terry Watson, Mike Whittingham, Melanie Wilkins OLY, Mark Zambarda

NOTES

Chapter 5

1. Lease's intervention led to Gardener eventually gaining a degree

Chapter 10

1. Matthew Hughey, Devon Goss: *A Level Playing Field? Media Constructions of Athletics, Genetics, and Race* - https://doi.org/10.1177/0002716215588067

Chapter 16

1. Matthew Syed: *Rebel Ideas: The Power of Diverse Thinking*
2. https://www.theguardian.com/sport/2012/aug/10/london-2012-great-britain-disqualified-relay

ALSO BY TRYSTAN BEVAN

'Brilliantly written and fascinating account of one of Britain's most successful athletes.'

'Darren Campbell is no ordinary athlete and this is no ordinary sports bio. Brutally honest and prepared to expose his inner demons both as an athlete and as a man, the book doesn't shy away from life's battles.'

'Sensitively written and a great look into what it takes to be an Olympic success.'

ALSO BY BEN MERCER

Such a great insight into the life of a professional rugby player.'

'If you're going to read one book on rugby, give the elite names a miss and read this.'

'Not just for anyone who's into rugby, but equally for anyone who can relate to the experience of living abroad.'

Printed in Great Britain
by Amazon

18973433R00130

THIS IS ME!

FUTURE VOICES

Edited By Byron Tobolik

First published in Great Britain in 2021 by:

YoungWriters
Est. 1991

Young Writers
Remus House
Coltsfoot Drive
Peterborough
PE2 9BF
Telephone: 01733 890066
Website: www.youngwriters.co.uk

Book Design by Ashley Janson

Softback ISBN 978-1-80015-680-7

Printed and bound in the UK by BookPrintingUK
Website: www.bookprintinguk.com
YB0489C

FOREWORD

For Young Writers' latest competition This Is Me, we asked primary school pupils to look inside themselves, to think about what makes them unique, and then write a poem about it! They rose to the challenge magnificently and the result is this fantastic collection of poems in a variety of poetic styles.

Here at Young Writers our aim is to encourage creativity in children and to inspire a love of the written word, so it's great to get such an amazing response, with some absolutely fantastic poems. It's important for children to focus on and celebrate themselves and this competition allowed them to write freely and honestly, celebrating what makes them great, expressing their hopes and fears, or simply writing about their favourite things. This Is Me gave them the power of words. The result is a collection of inspirational and moving poems that also showcase their creativity and writing ability.

I'd like to congratulate all the young poets in this anthology, I hope this inspires them to continue with their creative writing.

CONTENTS

Grace Jackson (10) 57
Daisy Doe (9) 58
Tay Clarke (10) 59
Henry Cook (9) 60
Alfie Craven (9) 61
Millie Rudd (9) 62
Chloé Rees (9) 63
Theodora Snowling (8) 64
Thomas Field (9) 65
George Banham-Crooks (9) 66
Maisie Davey (10) 67
Jack Bruce (9) 68
Joshua Wilde (9) 69
Rupert Meechan (8) 70
Ruby-Jean Hunt (8) 71
Daisy Conway (8) 72
Harriet Price (9) 73
George Watts (8) 74
Leopold Cossey (9) 75
Dillan Boden (10) 76
Willow Moore (9) 77
Covey Denton (9) 78
Lauren Crisp (9) 79

Hazlehurst Community Primary School, Ramsbottom

Oliver Hilton (10) 80
Jude Patric Doyle (10) 82
Ilithyia Crompton (10) 83
Isabella Berry (10) 84
Evan Shorland (11) 85
George Quinton (10) 86
Libby Stanley (10) 87
Eloise Ogden (10) 88
Ellie Connor-Hart (10) 89
Safir Agri (9) 90
Jamie Smith (10) 91
Grace Hardy (10) 92
Robbie Alston (10) 93
Jordan Snape (10) 94
Charlie Carroll (10) 95
Myles Templeton (10) 96
Keira Hardman (11) 97
Emily Barker (10) 98
Lilly Foster (10) 99
Emily Curry (10) 100
Scarlett Massingham (10) 101
Ava Carter (10) 102
Albert Burroughs (10) 103
Oliver Macadam (10) 104
Oscar Birkett (10) 105

Millbrook Community Primary School, Kirkby

Ava Winterson (9) 106
Alex McLean (9) 107
Amelia Alice Messham (9) 108
Millie Butler (9) 109
Michael Cormode (9) 110
Riley Grimes (9) 111

St Giles' & St George's CE Academy, Newcastle

Zain Muhammed (10) 112
Lucy Rowlands (10) 113
Dennis Jogy (10) 114
Elise Paige Goodwin (9) 115
Kai Virgo (10) 116
William Burton (9) 117
Jake Simpson (9) 118
Jack Austin (10) 119
Daniel Lambert (9) 120
Sorocco Saunders (9) 121
Scarlett Twigg (10) 122
Gracie Brace (9) 123
Saskia Roberts (9) 124
Rebecca Beesley (11) 125
Livvie Davies (9) 126
Leila Powner (10) 127
Milena Eardley (9) 128
Lacey Beeley (9) 129
Masyn Bowers (10) 130
Amelia Parton (9) 131
Eleanor Reader (9) 132
Petra-Talita Cozea (9) 133

THE POEMS

Happy And Lucky

H appiness is my favourite because when I am
happy, I am as kind as a nurse
A nd sweets are my favourite food, the red ones
are my favourite
P uppies are furry, fluffy, friendly and very little
P uppies need lots to eat and lots of energy
Y es, I have two puppies at home. One is ginger
and one is black

L ucky, I think I am lucky. I have a nice family
U sually, I have lots of presents on my birthday
C otton candy is my favourite, it is very nice and
fluffy
K ind, I have a gigantic, kind family
Y oung and full of life.

Annabelle Race (7)
Appleton Wiske CP School, Appleton Wiske

How To Make Me

What you will need:
Five pages of doodles.
A big bit of chocolate.
A lot of sprinkles.
Two pinches of fun.
8tsp of cheekiness.
Three caramel wafers.

How to do it:
First, add five pages of doodles and one milkshake.
Stir nicely.
Next, add two pinches of fun, a lot of sprinkles and three caramel wafers.
Whilst stirring, add a big bit of chocolate and add 8tsp of cheekiness.
Put it in the fridge and leave to cool. Then watch it bubble with fun.

Daisy Wilson (8)
Appleton Wiske CP School, Appleton Wiske

I Am Unique

I am as mischievous as a monkey,
When I see food, I am very hungry,
I love football and I play for a team,
I am emotional and passionate.

I am elegant like ballerinas,
I'm as loud as a house breaking down, *bash!*
I'm caring, cheerful and encouraging,
I'm also very educational.

When I am angry, I am a tiger,
I'm a perfectly insane mad person,
I am a kind, gentle, good-hearted girl,
I have two very annoying brothers.

Sophia Bateson (9)
Appleton Wiske CP School, Appleton Wiske

All About Me!

I am as fast as a falcon,
And I love being outdoors,
I like climbing anything,
And running across the moors.

I like playing music,
Do you do that too?
I am mostly vegetarian,
And I love going to the zoo.

I am a fennec fox,
People say I am good at sport,
My hair is very curly,
And I never get distraught.

I really like exploring,
Helping animals galore,
I really like being helpful,
And I only sometimes roar.

Joshua Ring (10)
Appleton Wiske CP School, Appleton Wiske

Only Me

Haiku poetry

Amazing archer,
I'm an awful acrobat,
Loud as a lion.

Angry like an ant,
Grumpy like a teacher (whoops),
I'm sometimes smiling.

I'm tough as old boots,
My hair is as soft as snow,
When red, I go *bang!*

I am a bomb, *boom!*
My haiku poem will end,
But I will live on.

Fierce as a lion,
I am very passionate,
Good ballerina.

When I have a task, I pursue it.

Dougal Gaudie (11)
Appleton Wiske CP School, Appleton Wiske

This Is Me

I love fluffy cats and bushy foxes,
I like making my cats things out of boxes,
Foxes have bushy tails,
Especially the big males,
I also like collecting Beanie Boos,
I like to cuddle them when I'm in a sleepy snooze,
I have so many I cannot count,
Because I have such a large amount,
Pasta is my favourite food,
Like my kitten, it puts me in a good mood,
My favourite drink is fizzy coke,
It always makes me think of a joke.

Beatrix Dyke (9)
Appleton Wiske CP School, Appleton Wiske

My Hamster Cookie

G ood at writing
R ight at some things
E ating is great
A mazing at swimming
T ikTok is a great app

H amsters are the best
A dventurous and friendly
M y hamster is called Cookie
S illy and as kind as a nurse
T he Impossible is the best movie
E aster is my favourite thing
R uns as fast as a tiger.

Lily Easby (8)
Appleton Wiske CP School, Appleton Wiske

How To Be Me

What you will need:
Lots of flexibility.
One pinch of mischief.
A slice of chocolate.
A dash of fun.
Plus, a lot of pizza.

How to do it:
First, get a bowl and mix in the flexibility for about five minutes.
Next, add in the pinch of mischief and mix well until stretchy and fluffy like a puppy.
Lastly, add a lot of pizza and then you are finished.

Erin Mulholland (8)
Appleton Wiske CP School, Appleton Wiske

This Is Me

Sometimes I am funny,
And as bouncy as a bunny,
I am always kind,
So I am not fined.

I love every type of dog,
And getting muddy in a bog,
I am always loud,
And sometimes a bit proud.

I am a tiger as I stroll through the house,
And sometimes spot a minute mouse,
I brush my long, brown hair,
As I watch birds fly through the air.

Sophie Elizabeth Elizabeth Green (10)
Appleton Wiske CP School, Appleton Wiske

As Fierce As A Lion

As fierce as a lion,
Sometimes a bit too much,
I am as cunning as a fox,
I'm a monkey, I am so wild.

As fierce as a lion,
I am very friendly,
I am a bomb. *Bang!* I go off,
My mum says I'm good, I smile.

As fierce as a lion,
As mood as a mule,
I can be angry if I want,
I am as tough as an old boot.

Rosie Wilson (10)
Appleton Wiske CP School, Appleton Wiske

I Am Unique

I have plaited brown hair,
And greeny-blue eyes,
My plaits touch my chair,
And I am always organised.

I am as high as a kite,
And I am always kind,
I am always polite,
A nicer person you won't find.

I also adore reading,
And I love climbing trees,
My dogs always need feeding,
And I sometimes scrape my knees.

Poppy Race (10)

Appleton Wiske CP School, Appleton Wiske

This Is Me

T his is me
H aving fun with my dog is the best
I love my mum, she is nicer than a nurse
S o is my dog Ella, she is cuter than a cat

I love my dad, he is strong
S ulky Kassi is a nurse

M y brother is mad like my BFF
E lla is my dog's name, she is cheeky.

Zak Sanerivi (7)
Appleton Wiske CP School, Appleton Wiske

Me

I am a mountain biker,
But I am sometimes a hiker,
I do not have much money,
And I don't like honey.

I am a bed cover huddler,
And a dog cuddler,
I am a monkey,
And quite funky.

Lego constructor,
Sausage roll abductor,
I am as loud as lightning,
And don't like writing.

John Robert Havelock Roe (9)
Appleton Wiske CP School, Appleton Wiske

This Is Me

G reat at reading
R eally, writing is my favourite
A mazing gymnast
C areful writing
E pic stuff in my life

B rilliant at gymnastics
E ven better at skipping
L oves to be helpful
L oves to be kind.

Grace Bell (7)
Appleton Wiske CP School, Appleton Wiske

All About Me

I feel like a bird on my horse,
When I go over a jump,
I am flying through the air,
Galloping across the field,
Walking around with lots of joy.

I'm a rocket, galloping everywhere,
Jumping over fences,
One very friendly horse,
Saddle so comfy.

Ellie McGuigan (9)
Appleton Wiske CP School, Appleton Wiske

Haiden Patel

Haiku poetry

I like Mum and Dad,
I really like my cat too,
I like my fish too.

I don't like peanuts,
I do not like risotto,
I do hate black beans.

I do not mind school,
I do not mind paired reading,
I don't mind spiders.

Haiden Patel (10)

Appleton Wiske CP School, Appleton Wiske

Fun Snow Girl

Haiku poetry

I can dance and prance,
Glistening ice, all things pleasant,
I can glow with snow.

I can be angry,
I can be massively loud,
As loud as a bomb.

I am glittering,
And most of all, I am fun,
I love snow, snow, snow.

Violet Rose Ellison (9)

Appleton Wiske CP School, Appleton Wiske

My Favourite Animal

Cute and cuddly,
Warm and soft,
Fast like a Ferrari,
Slower than a train,
Fits in any tiny spot,
Bites harder than a hammer,
Sharper than a knife.
What is it?

Answer: A land shark.

Eva Mae Pearce (8)
Appleton Wiske CP School, Appleton Wiske

Rainbow Me

Red, my stepdad is really funny and makes me laugh a lot.
Orange, my bestie is kind and amazing, she always helps me when I'm upset.
Yellow, my mum is happy, hardworking and positive.
Green, my dog really enjoys barking and being pushed in my little sister's pushchair.
Blue, my brother is really noisy, especially on Minecraft.
Indigo, my sister is really cute and has a beautiful smile.
Violet, I really love my family, they make me feel whole and as colourful as a rainbow!

Sofia Redfern (10)
Bassingham Primary School, Bassingham

Rainbow And Lightning, Clouds And Sunshine

Sometimes I'm happy, kind, jolly, lovely, helpful,
friendly and I have a lovely smile.

Sometimes I'm angry, anxious, scared, worried,
negative, sad and I have a nasty frown.

Sometimes I argue with my sister, but really I love
her.
When we fall out I am mad, but when we make up
I am glad.

My dog is my favourite. Whenever I am sad, he
comes.
He has a great big smile and grin to light up the
day.

Safia King (10)
Bassingham Primary School, Bassingham

My Class

Brave, artistic, exploring the world,
Out of control, nurturing, awesome,
Good fisherman, sporty, competitive,
Daredevil, cute, legendary, timid,
Imaginative, cricketer, happy bee,
Love animals, hotshot, silver gym,
Rock model, awesome drawer, arty,
Caring, overcoming fear,
Good at sewing, silver karate, goldy.

I love my class, it's great.

Reuben Taylor (10)
Bassingham Primary School, Bassingham

Ingredients Of Me

This is me,
I am unique.
Just like a snowflake,
Here's what makes me, me.

I love my family,
More than anything.
They make me feel calm,
I have loads of fun.
What would I do without them?

Sprinkle a bit of running,
Dump a lot of football,
Add a teaspoon full of kindness,
And that's what makes me, me!

Harrison Jones (10)
Bassingham Primary School, Bassingham

This Is Me!

Dinosaurs, dogs and dingos,
Really are my thing,
But what I like most of all is...
Purple, blue and pink.
I am brave,
But I wish I could explore a cave.
I am very energetic,
When the clock goes *tick-tock, tick-tock!*
Helpful and happy is what I am,
Especially when I eat ham or jam.
I am me,
As happy as can be.

Eliza Cotton (10)

Bassingham Primary School, Bassingham

I Am Me!

I am happy and useful,
Clever and fast,
This is me.

I am friendly and sneaky,
Lucky and strong,
This is me.

I am competitive and quiet,
Skilled and imaginative,
This is me.

I am funny and organised,
Wise and artistic,
I am me and I am unique!

Dylan Taylor (10)

Bassingham Primary School, Bassingham

This Is Me

U nique
N ice
I ndependent
Q ueen at TikTok
U nder my heart, I love my family
E ntertaining

I 'm pretty
S o helpful
O rganised
B eing happy
E nergetic
L aughter.

Isobel Chapman (10)
Bassingham Primary School, Bassingham

The Ingredients To Make Me

Xbox, Fortnite, football and YouTube = me.
When I was in lockdown, I practically lived on technology.
Schoolwork was not fun, but screentime was.

Playing Splitgate is fun.
Football is fun.
Family and friends are really fun.

Isaac Taylor (10)
Bassingham Primary School, Bassingham

My Name's Henley

H ome is where I rest
E very day, I try to have fun
N early every day, I play football
L ong days at school
E very month, I go jet-skiing
Y es, these things are me!

Henley Fox (11)
Bassingham Primary School, Bassingham

Hayden!

H appiest playing Minecraft
A wesome at Roblox
Y ellow is one of my favourite colours
D rawing is my favourite hobby
E specially creative
N ow I want an axolotl.

Hayden Drury (11)
Bassingham Primary School, Bassingham

This Is Me!

G reat at gymnastics
Y ou are unique
M y dream
N ever give up
A thletic
S uper artistic
T his is me.

Lucca John Sheppard (10)
Bassingham Primary School, Bassingham

This Is Me

I love Fortnite,
My mum is amazing,
My mum is fantastic at her job,
My nana is the best nana ever,
Fortnite is great,
Tennis is amazingly good.

Kyan Mack (10)
Bassingham Primary School, Bassingham

Who Am I?

I am a magician.
I am Argentinian,
And the GOAT at football.
I am 5'7" and 35.
Who am I?

Answer: Lionel Messi.

Ryan Bracher (10)

Bassingham Primary School, Bassingham

Ikram Is My Name

Ikram is my name and I am not ashamed to say,
My hair is puffier and fluffier than a sheep's wool.
Speaking of sheep, I love them,
They're cuddlier than a teddy bear.
I love to cook, it's in my blood,
And I have three best buds.
Whenever I'm at restaurants, pizza is my go-to,
And I fill my belly up to the brim,
Sometimes I overflow, but that's just what I do.
I love reading my Dork Diaries,
And love watching YouTube,
But what I love the most is my family.
Ikram is my name and I am not ashamed to say,
My hair is puffier and fluffier than a sheep's wool.

Ikram Olayiwola (9)
Broughton Fields Primary School, Broughton

How To Make An Exquisite Me: Anah

Ingredients to make Anah:
100 gallons of a cat lover.
A pinch of adventure.
10% of energy flour.
A splash of self-confidence.
10g of smartness.
100g of kindness and helpfulness.

Now you need to:
Put 10g of smartness and 10% of energy flour in a bowl.
Stir until it's watery, then add a splash of self-confidence, 100g of kindness and helpfulness and 100 gallons of a cat lover and stir again.
Finally, a pinch of adventure, then put it in the oven for one hour.

That's me, Anah!

Anah Lafir (9)
Broughton Fields Primary School, Broughton

How To Make Precious Me!

Follow every step!

You will need:
A pour of joyfulness.
A sprinkle of sadness.
A lot of pizza.
Lots and lots of books that send my imagination wilder than a lion.
A splash of green.
A dust of confidence.

How to make me:
First: Grab a large bucket and gush the joyfulness down.
Second: Sprinkle the sadness into the mixture.
Third: Add the pizza and books, and stir.
Fourth: Add the green and confidence.
Now stir and enjoy having fun!

Hameeda Sumaila (9)
Broughton Fields Primary School, Broughton

The Really Cool Rap Poem

I am a player, I like gaming.
I like pandas and human beings.
I have an Xbox and I am chilled,
You'll be gasping when I beat you ten nil.
I like pixel graphics, they're my fave,
Guess what game I play and I won't hate.
I like to be creative and give out motives.
I like PvP more than building.
Don't teach me how to play,
'Cos I'm good enough to be competing.
I'm a super intense Minecraft player.

Erny Kohhantsuk (9)
Broughton Fields Primary School, Broughton

Darci

There was a sloth loving girl,
Who I think lives in this world,
And she loves chicken nuggets,
More than gold in a bucket,
Her best friend is Jade,
And she hates being called a maid,
This girl spends her time gaming,
But she's quite bad when it comes to naming,
She spends her time reading,
But while she tries to pick out a sweet candy cane,
The store owner accidentally exposes her name...
"Darci!"

Darci Jefferies (9)
Broughton Fields Primary School, Broughton

Me And My Family

My name is Alice, my age is small.
I live in a house with a door that you have to open to enter, but knock on it first.
When you enter, you will see my mum cooking and my dad will normally be snoozing.
You will hear my brother shouting as he plays his game or he will be deeply asleep in his room.
Then, at last, you will see me all cuddled up in bed with my cat all snuggled up beside me.
So now you know all about my family!

Alice Lalina (9)
Broughton Fields Primary School, Broughton

I Am Kaylan

I am a kind friend because I help people.
I am a sporty kid because I play football.
I love animals.
I am a pizza lover.
I am a chicken nugget lover.
I am a shoe lover.
I am a paper plane lover.
I am a bull lover.
I am a pumpkin picker.
I am a Freddie lover as he is my friend.
I am a tennis lover.
I am a cheese lover.
I am a pepperoni lover.
I am a Spider-Man lover kid.

Kaylan Card (9)
Broughton Fields Primary School, Broughton

About Me

T ravelling around the world exploring
H ave a brother or sister?
I have a brother and a sister
S ometimes they annoy me, but I stay calm

I love going for cycles because I'm a sporty kid
S ometimes I go by myself, but sometimes I go
with my brother

M y favourite food is pizza
E xpect that I'll always be out cycling.

Sajjad Muraj (9)
Broughton Fields Primary School, Broughton

This Is Me

I am an intense Minecraft player and a good gamer,
A good shamer and a good football player.
I am a good game, not a rager,
Because I am a chilled gamer.
I am a good helper and a good roaster,
I will roast you like one, two, three like baby steps.
That's what my dog can do,
Dogs, I love them, especially my dog,
He's loving, cute and really happy.

Harvey Lambert (9)
Broughton Fields Primary School, Broughton

Me And My Family

My name is Ivine,
I move like a python.
I am very tiring,
But also inspiring.
I have a little sister,
She is annoying,
But also so joyful.
My mum is always cooking,
But my dad is always snooping.
I am gaming,
But not bailing.
I am a witch,
But not a snitch.
I do like to ditch,
But not if there's a snitch.

Ivine Pobee (9)
Broughton Fields Primary School, Broughton

School Poem

I have some friends to play with at school.
We don't have homework and the school is fun.
We read books, play, and do maths and writing.
Everything is so easy and my teacher is nice and fun.
Our studies are nice and good fun.
They talk very well and read so very well.
Lunch is good and I have so much food and drink.

Aubrey Leung (10)
Broughton Fields Primary School, Broughton

How To Spell Brian

B rian is so brilliant!
R esilience, Brian is resilient like a tiger!
I nspirational, Brian is so incredibly inspirational
A spirations, Brian has aspirations and is super amazing
N ice, Brian is so nice, ten times nicer than every nurse in the world!

My name is... Brian.

Brian Agyemang (9)
Broughton Fields Primary School, Broughton

This Is All About Me

I'm loving,
I'm brave,
I'm kind,
I'm sporty,
I'm awesome,
I'm curious,
I like going on bike rides,
My favourite colour is lime green,
I'm adventurous,
I'm chilled,
I'm smart,
My name is Kailan,
This is me.

Kailan Smart (9)
Broughton Fields Primary School, Broughton

How To Make Me

How to make me:
Fill me up with bravery and smartness.
Put in 100lbs of happiness and kindness.
Put in 60g of helping homeless people and helping everyone like teachers and people just like you.
Put in 200% of loving rock climbing.

And that's me!

Maria Mckenzie (10)
Broughton Fields Primary School, Broughton

How To Bake A Thea Jackson

To make me, you will need...
To pour in a three-litre jug of kindness,
Weigh out 15kg of adventurous,
Stir in two dollops of inventiveness,
Add a 2,000-litre jug of animal love,
Sieve in eight handfuls of hilariousness,
Slice up some gentleness,
Dice up some support,
A splash of peacefulness,
Stir in a drop of intelligence,
A tablespoon of loving,
A cup of caring,
Mix in some respectfulness,
Pour in a two-litre cup of wiseness,
Sprinkle in some friendliness,
Chop up some loyalty,
And bake till the 23rd of May.
(Best before: 23rd May, 2023!)

Thea Jackson (8)
Hainford VC Primary School, Hainford

How To Make Me!

First, you need to:
Start with a base of visionary, dip in some foxy sprinkles and leave to set until the 4th of January.
Secondly...
Add half a spoon of assiduous and stir for three minutes.
After that...
Sieve in a few grams of wondrous and remove any annoying sauce from the mixture, then stir.
To garnish...
Sprinkle on some amusement, add a handful of beloved and leave to set for ten years. Make sure to take it out of the fridge before it goes stale!
Eat with a packet of dexterous, a pinch of astonishing, and enjoy!

Matilda Price (10)
Hainford VC Primary School, Hainford

The Lovely Pearl Bridgeman

I'm as hungry as a llama in a car.
I'm as young as a newborn fish.
I'm as tall as a giraffe kneeling down.
I'm as clever as a monkey using a phone.
I'm as wild as a horse galloping around.
I'm as fun as a playful puppy.
I'm as flimsy as a rubber band.
I'm as protective as a mother bird.
I'm as daring as an adventurer.
I'm as pretty as a pearl.
I'm as friendly as a growing kitten.
I'm as funny as my friends Ruby and Bella.
I'm as bright as the shining sun.

Pearl Bridgeman (9)
Hainford VC Primary School, Hainford

How To Bake An Ellie Rudd

How to bake an Ellie Rudd:
First of all, apply your gloves and apron,
As this can get messy!
First of all, pour in a jug of judicious,
And don't forget a dollop of ingenious.
Add in a handful of awe-inspiring,
And a splash of stupefying!
Next, the decorations:
Sprinkle on some merry,
And now it's almost ready!
Bake for ten years,
But wait!
Finish baking and eat within one second!
I just hope you read the instructions properly...

Ellie Rudd (10)
Hainford VC Primary School, Hainford

I Am As Strong As Oak

I'm as strong as an oak,
I'm as fierce as a holly bush,
I'm as wild as ivy,
I'm as curious as a cat,
I'm as playful as a puppy,
I'm as flimsy as a squirrel,
I'm as clumsy as an elephant,
I'm as pinchy as a crab,
I'm as clever as a monkey,
I'm as protective as a mother bear,
I'm as loud as a roaring lion,
I'm as funny as a hyena,
I'm as creative as a flower,
I'm as friendly as a lamb.

Isabella Bedington (9)
Hainford VC Primary School, Hainford

Merryn

To make Merryn, you have to:
Of course, add a dollop of madness,
Apply a jug of sticky, icky curious syrup,
Slice up some ludicrous,
Sprinkle in immediately fine flour,
A splash of brainy water,
Drop in some crackerjack serum,
Add four drops of dexterous,
Apply 500g of originality,
Add a spoonful of creativity,
Bake for ten years.
Best before:
1st August, 2011.

Warning: Poisonous, don't eat!

Merryn Britcher (10)
Hainford VC Primary School, Hainford

How To Bake An Amelia

To bake an Amelia, you need to:
Add some consideration,
Pour in some compassion,
Add a spoonful of originality,
Sprinkle in some support,
Splash in a handful of ludicrous,
Mix in some faith,
Chop up some understanding,
Slice some social,
Sprinkle in some magnificence,
Stir in some visionary,
Weigh out some inventiveness,
Then cook some till February 13th,
But you'll only have one day for it.

Amelia Banham (10)
Hainford VC Primary School, Hainford

How To Bake A Toby Spears!

First, you need to:
Add a jug of humdinger,
Splash in rapid-fire flow,
Crack in three visionary eggs,
Pour in half a jug of boisterous milk.

Now for decoration:
Dollop on some mind-blowing sprinkles,
Chop up 200g of knowledgeable carrots,
Plop on some advantageous Maltesers,
Finally, add some foxy icing to the top,
Then bake it in the oven for ten whole years!
Enjoy!

Toby Spears (10)
Hainford VC Primary School, Hainford

How To Bake An Elsa Jackson

To bake an Elsa Jackson, you need to:
Add four tablespoons of adorableness,
A jug of hilariousness,
Weigh out 1kg of intelligence,
Mix in some logical syrup,
Add a splash of welcoming,
Dollop 600g of entertaining,
Sieve in some kind-hearted flour,
Decorate with five tablespoons of pleasantness,
Stir ten times clockwise,
And bake on the 1st March.

Elsa Jackson (10)
Hainford VC Primary School, Hainford

How To Bake A Sienna Edwards

First, you will need a bowl, obviously,
Then add a cup full of confidence,
A jug full of originality,
Then add a pinch of craziness,
Then add a spoonful of gifted,
Don't forget a slice of friendship!
Then add a handful of bravery,
Four litres of powerful,
Mix with seven grams of entertaining,
Then add to the rest of the mixture and bake for ten years.

Sienna Edwards (10)
Hainford VC Primary School, Hainford

How To Bake An Iced Ellie Bruce

Start by...
Dunking in some inventiveness,
Then add a spoonful of amusement,
Next, sieve in some adventure,
After that, pour in some thoughtfulness,
Now weigh out 10kg of wisdom and add it in,
Next, sprinkle on some craziness,
Now wait until September 3rd and bake for nine years.
(But make sure you eat it before the 20th of September.)

Ellie Bruce (9)
Hainford VC Primary School, Hainford

How To Bake A Grace Jackson

To bake a Grace Jackson, you will first need to...
Add two cups of kindness,
A splash of funniness,
Stir in a cup of loyalty,
Sieve in a cup of creativity,
Sprinkle in a bit of inventiveness,
Last ingredient, dip in a spoonful of skills.
Finally, bake for ten years.
Also, it expires on the 5th August, 2011.

Grace Jackson (10)
Hainford VC Primary School, Hainford

How To Bake A Daisy Doe

First, add 100g of hard work into a large bowl,
Then add a splash of learning,
After that, chop up a handful of love,
Add a dollop of wonder,
Add a slice of pride,
Stir in some joy,
Sift in some laughter,
Drop in some intelligence,
And finally, bake for nine years,
Eat before nine seconds,
Done. Enjoy!

Daisy Doe (9)
Hainford VC Primary School, Hainford

How To Make A Tay Cupcake...

First, add a teensy-weensy spoon full of impressiveness,
Secondly, add a mega jug of silliness,
Next, add 1kg of rapid-fire,
Then add a mega, mega jug of strength,
And then a splash of awesomeness,
After that, add a drop of amusement,
And finally, add a teensy-weensy drop of kindness,
Bake until March 6th.

Tay Clarke (10)
Hainford VC Primary School, Hainford

How To Bake A Henry Cook

First, you need a bowl,
Next, add...
A dollop of sportiness,
A teaspoon of strength,
Mix in some kindness,
A cup of daring,
Sprinkle on some wiseness,
Sieve in some swiftness,
Sprinkle on some respect,
Stir in some OP gaming,
Cook for eight hours.
Best before September the 16th.

Henry Cook (9)
Hainford VC Primary School, Hainford

All About Me

I am as funny as a kangaroo with a baby rabbit
wearing a clown costume and fuzzy, pink
Christmas slippers.
I am as smart as an elephant.
I am as loving as a panda with her cubs.
I am as fast as a purple and yellow monkey
wearing roller skates.
I am a caring as Spider-Man helping an old lady
cross the road.

Alfie Craven (9)
Hainford VC Primary School, Hainford

To Make A Millie

To make a Millie, you need...
A splash of weirdness,
Add a normal slice of kindness,
A dollop of dumbness (must weigh one gram),
Mix in,
Bake for nine seconds,
Sprinkle on a bit of creativity,
Wait nine years for it cool down,
It will expire on July 20th,
Enjoy.

Millie Rudd (9)
Hainford VC Primary School, Hainford

How To Bake A Chloé

To bake me, you will need...
A jug of caring,
A slice of wisdom,
A dollop of knowledge,
A cup of kindness,
A handful of inspiration,
A spoonful of beauty,
A bagful of accommodation,
A teaspoon of clumsiness,
A bowl of humour,
Best before the 6th September.

Chloé Rees (9)
Hainford VC Primary School, Hainford

How To Bake A Teddy Snowling

This is the recipe to bake a Teddy...
First, add a jug of brilliance,
Add a slice of nobody's fool,
A handful of inspiration,
Mix in a bit of knowledge,
A cup of well-knowing maths.

P.S. Best before 26th July, 2022,
Bake until Novermber 1st.

Theodora Snowling (8)
Hainford VC Primary School, Hainford

How To Bake A Thomas Field

Firstly, add a jug of imagination,
Then sprinkle in some kindness,
Dollop in 5kg of creativity,
Mix in some friendship,
Drop in 2kg of smartness,
Decorate with slices of strength,
Splash in 10kg of chatterbox,
Eat in nine years,
(It could go stale.)

Thomas Field (9)
Hainford VC Primary School, Hainford

How To Bake A Cake Of Me

A crunch of speed,
A splash of wiseness,
Two drops of liveliness,
A cup of skills,
A glass of slyness,
A piece of swiftness,
A piece of happiness,
A slice of kindness,
A jug of pleasantness,
It is ready,
Go bake the cake for eight years.

George Banham-Crooks (9)
Hainford VC Primary School, Hainford

How To Bake A Maisie Davey...

To bake a Maisie Davey, you need to:
Sprinkle in a spoonful of creativity,
Pour a jug full of kindness,
Drop in a dollop of bravery,
Mix in some loyalty,
Add a sprinkle of skills,
Then bake it on the 30th September,
And eat it in ten years.

Maisie Davey (10)
Hainford VC Primary School, Hainford

How To Build A Jack...

First glue a little bit of intelligence,
Sew in a little bit of kindness,
Tape on a bit of fun,
Then weld on a bit of caring,
Attach a little bit of helpfulness,
Dip it in a big bit of funniness,
Stick on a bit of emotion,
Let it dry for nine years.

Jack Bruce (9)
Hainford VC Primary School, Hainford

How To Make A Josh

You will need:
A cupful of giftedness,
A jug of diligence,
A spoonful of wiseness,
A spoonful of cleverness,
A cup of fun,
A spoonful of speediness,
A splash of friendliness,
Bake on the 19th of March.

Joshua Wilde (9)
Hainford VC Primary School, Hainford

How To Bake A Rupert

First put in a bowl of golf skills,
Add a jug of friendliness,
Put in a teaspoon of clumsiness,
Add a dollop of sportsmanship,
Put in two litres of tractor knowledge,
Mix in a slice of friendship,
Bake for eight years.

Rupert Meechan (8)
Hainford VC Primary School, Hainford

This Is Ruby-Jean

I am as lazy as a dog lying on a log.
I am as weird as a bat chewing on a hat.
I am as small as a mouse in your house.
I am as fit as an axolotl swimming in a bottle.
I am as cute as a goat on mute.
I am as cool as a pool.

Ruby-Jean Hunt (8)
Hainford VC Primary School, Hainford

Daisy Is...

I am as smart as a cat, but as blind as a bat.
I am as tall as a giraffe nibbling on some grass.
I am as funny as a monkey peeling a banana.
I am as crazy as a puppy that's ready to play.
I am as weird as a frog with a hat.

Daisy Conway (8)
Hainford VC Primary School, Hainford

This Is Me, Harriet Price

I am as beautiful as an elegant swan,
I am as clumsy as a wobbly jelly,
I am as funny as a dancing dog,
I am as friendly as a cuddly kitten,
I am as smart as Albert Einstein,
And I am as helpful as a hardworking builder.

Harriet Price (9)
Hainford VC Primary School, Hainford

How To Bake Me: A Cake Of Me

To make me:
A jug of bravery,
A handful of laughter,
A slice of kindness,
A splash of supportiveness,
A cupful of wisdom,
A spoonful of silliness,
A dollop of welcoming,
Bake for eight years.

George Watts (8)
Hainford VC Primary School, Hainford

A Me Cake

To bake a Leopold Cossey, you need to add:
18kg of understanding,
A spoonful of intelligence,
Stir in some swiftness,
A splash of giftedness,
A sprinkle of cooperation,
Finally, bake for nine minutes.

Leopold Cossey (9)
Hainford VC Primary School, Hainford

How To Bake A Dillan

Add 100g of microscopic,
One jug of funniness,
Sprinkle in a bit of gutsy,
Stir in some delicateness,
Sieve in some playfulness,
Splash in a bit of boisterousness,
On the second of May, bake it for 11 years.

Dillan Boden (10)
Hainford VC Primary School, Hainford

How To Bake A Willow Moore

You will need:
A spoonful of creativity,
A splash of kindness,
Add in a jug of cheerfulness,
Stir in some smiles,
Chop up some greatness,
Sprinkle on some peace,
Then bake for nine years.

Willow Moore (9)
Hainford VC Primary School, Hainford

Shopping List For Covey

A jug of grit,
A bottle of preciousness,
A splash of love,
A kilo of silliness,
A box of friendship,
A packet of wisdom,
It will be done on the 18th of May.

Covey Denton (9)
Hainford VC Primary School, Hainford

How To Bake A Lauren Crisp...

Add a spoonful of intelligence,
Add a cupful of kindness,
Stir in some graciousness,
A jug full of diligence,
Then bake for nine years.

Lauren Crisp (9)
Hainford VC Primary School, Hainford

A Pea Life

Every morning, I wake up squished,
So hard between my brothers and sisters,
I think I'm about to pop.
As I squeeze out of the pod,
I land on the ground with a bob.
As I steadily get to my feet,
My brothers and sisters fall out,
Leaving me underneath.
As they all rush off,
One of my sisters sees a frog.
As we all run away,
I think, *I don't want to be the football today,*
But no, I'm too slow.
They kick me, hit me and throw me too,
I feel like I'm flowing through the clouds and to the sky I zoom.
Finally, when they leave for the day, I bury my head in the soil and mutter the same words as yesterday,
"I'll run away someday,
To a place far away,

Where the grass grows green and the trees sway longingly,"
As I lean over this wonderful place I know I'm protected behind Mother Nature's big green gates.

Oliver Hilton (10)

Hazlehurst Community Primary School, Ramsbottom

This Is Me

Hi guys, my name is Jude,
I've got a weird life as I'm no ordinary dude.
I started playing the violin, but everyone else quit,
They couldn't have loved it one little bit!
But I kept on going and I did quite well,
I told you people, but they thought I fell.
I did once, literally, straight on my toe,
I wanted help and got it, but instantly? No.
I liked music, so I started playing the cornet, guitar and piano,
So much that I even made musical models of playdough.
Do you think I'm done? Just music and pain?
Well, think again!
I am ten years old and a good worker,
My life could be good, but that's not my only purpose.
I have a lot of friends, some better than others,
And I have enemies too, but I'm just tougher!
And here's the bit that will make you gape,
Me and my friends are all crazy and huddle in a big heap!

Jude Patric Doyle (10)
Hazlehurst Community Primary School, Ramsbottom

A Recipe For Me

You need:
A pinch of kindness,
A dash of food,
A handful of happiness,
Some cakes and cookies,
A lot of animals,
Lots of colour,
And last but not least...
A bunch of good best friends,
And a cupful of family.

Method:
Firstly, you take the dash of food and a lot of animals and mix.
Secondly, you add lots of colour.
Thirdly, you mix in the cakes and cookies and a pinch of kindness.
Last but not least, add in a bunch of best friends and a cupful of family.
That's how you make me!

Ilithyia Crompton (10)
Hazlehurst Community Primary School, Ramsbottom

About Me!

I really hope that my anxiety goes away,
I am proud of going as fast as a rocket,
On my shiny metal (shaped as a bike) with grippy wheels.
Ilithyia, Evie and I are best friends.
My favourite colour is green, just like nature.
I am happy with my curly, brown, cute dog.
Ilithyia and I play outside in our spare time.
I like to let my wild adventures go free,
On some paper like a light cloud.
My family are amazing people to spend time with.
That's all about me!

Isabella Berry (10)
Hazlehurst Community Primary School, Ramsbottom

Washing Up Sucks

Washing up, tell me about it!
Scrubbing the dirty, rotten plates,
Who knows what's on them?
Poison? Mould? Vegetables?
Random stuff stuck there like Blu Tack (probably alive),
The pans are a different story,
Beans, I think, get stuck to the side,
And I don't think the pan was red and black when we bought it,
I'm scrubbing so hard that the bristles fall off,
My point is...
Washing up sucks.

Evan Shorland (11)
Hazlehurst Community Primary School, Ramsbottom

A Recipe For Me

First, add 5kg of goalkeeper skills.
Second, add 1lb of controllers, mics and a console.
Next, add 6kg of extraordinary swimming skills.
After that, add 10kg of a crazy, mad dog.
Finally, add 30kg of a crazy, mad family.
Now whisk everything together until liquidy.
Next, pour all the mixture into a cake tin and put it into the oven at 60°C for 30 minutes.

George Quinton (10)
Hazlehurst Community Primary School, Ramsbottom

My Dog Friend

My friend might be a dog, but he is the love of my life,
He's been there for me, from time to time, since 2016.
When he was as small as a mouse, he made me smile,
He can jump as high as the Hilton in Manchester.
When I'm not there, his eyes are as blue as the ocean,
His name is Billy and he can be silly.
When I'm sad, Billy is always in my heart.

Libby Stanley (10)
Hazlehurst Community Primary School, Ramsbottom

All About Me

I'm as gentle as a gazelle in a dance studio.
In studs, I'm as rapid as a cheetah.
I shoot at every opportunity.
I love the colour of the sea.
The seven siblings that I have, I love with all my heart,
My parents and grandparents, I'll love till the end,
I love my furry pet called Hamey,
And my friends from inside and outside of school.

Eloise Ogden (10)
Hazlehurst Community Primary School, Ramsbottom

I Am Karate Girl!

Karate is my thing,
Especially when I am in the ring.
I am the friendliest owner of the feistiest cat in town,
He likes to give me cuddles when I'm a tiny bit down.
I love Marvel a lot,
Especially when there's a good plot.
Pizza is elite,
Just like a sweet treat.
My family are the best,
Just like tomato pasta.
This is me.

Ellie Connor-Hart (10)
Hazlehurst Community Primary School, Ramsbottom

All About Me

S uper
A nimal lover
F riendly
I nquisitive
R espectful

A mazing
G uinea pigs
R eally fun
I am Safir

Kind, nice, good with animals
Gets into rambles
Likes to play
Every day
I like the outdoors
To take pictures
That's why I am me.

Safir Agri (9)
Hazlehurst Community Primary School, Ramsbottom

Amazing Me

I am the colourful rainbow that will shine on you.
I am the biggest controller of all time.
I am the smiling dog on your street.
My favourite Yum Yum is the triangle dough with toppings and the boiled and cut potato chips,
And there's nothing better than caring for the one that gave me life,
I am most happy with what I get.
Amazing me.

Jamie Smith (10)
Hazlehurst Community Primary School, Ramsbottom

I Am Me

I am a horse rider, I love horses.
I am a rabbit owner, Buttons is the best.
I am an Anglesey visitor, it's the best place for a holiday.
I am a forest wanderer, the most peaceful place.
I am a dog keeper, Eric loves to bark.
I am an ocean swimmer and I jump over the waves.
I am a nature seeker, flower power!

Grace Hardy (10)
Hazlehurst Community Primary School, Ramsbottom

About Me

I am the proudest owner of the waggiest tail in the whole wide world,
And I love him with my whole heart.

I am a big fan of flipping the exciting new pages,
I love the dripping sauce that goes with the twirly ingredients.

My favourite sweets are Skittles,
My favourite colour is blue.

Robbie Alston (10)
Hazlehurst Community Primary School, Ramsbottom

Funny, Fabulous Me

A kennings poem

I am...
A friend seeker,
A fun maker,
An adventure enjoyer,
A fun guy (not a mushroom!),
An epic gamer,
A sunset watcher,
A stick collector,
A tree admirer,
A comedy creator,
A bear hugger,
A family lover,
And most importantly...
An incredible person.

Jordan Snape (10)
Hazlehurst Community Primary School, Ramsbottom

This Is Me

I am a lightning midfielder,
Adventure books are where I escape to a wilder life.
I need to get faster to run through the defence,
It is hard to run through brick walls to get to the net.
My dog is called Peggy and she is very crazy,
But sometimes, she is very lazy.

Charlie Carroll (10)
Hazlehurst Community Primary School, Ramsbottom

This Is Me

A kennings poem

A FIFA demolisher,
A confident footballer,
A pet lover,
My favourite colour: Red,
A KFC lover,
A dog walker,
A book reader,
A water drinker,
A big laugher,
A speedy runner,
A hugging machine,
A healthy human being.
This is me.

Myles Templeton (10)
Hazlehurst Community Primary School, Ramsbottom

It's Only Me!

I am a...
Fiesty food eater,
Amazing adventurer,
Ambitious archaeologist,
Relaxing reader,
Steady swimmer,
Pet wanter,
Frequent procrastinator,
And finally...
A brilliant person who is very lucky.

Keira Hardman (11)
Hazlehurst Community Primary School, Ramsbottom

This Is Just Me

My dog Frankie makes me happy,
Although he is very yappy.
My cat is very silly,
And her name is Tilly.
I wish to be a vet,
But I'm not there yet.
I am so loud,
But I am also very proud.

Emily Barker (10)
Hazlehurst Community Primary School, Ramsbottom

Me

A kennings poem

Myth seeker,
Crystal hunter,
Chocolate muncher,
Wolf admirer,
Pizza eater,
Marvel watcher,
Siberian husky lover,
Cake baker,
Master drawer,
And finally,
A brilliant helper.

Lilly Foster (10)
Hazlehurst Community Primary School, Ramsbottom

All About Me

A kennings poem

I am a...
Pet carer,
Mini Vera,
Fun bringer,
Mum cuddler,
Dad hugger,
Geography lover,
Amazing singer,
Lettuce craver,
And finally,
A brilliant helper.

Emily Curry (10)
Hazlehurst Community Primary School, Ramsbottom

I Am!

A kennings poem

I am a...
Book reader,
Fajita eater,
Dog lover,
Football player,
Person helper.
Story writer,
Maths lover,
Friend maker,
Finally...
I am a good person.

Scarlett Massingham (10)
Hazlehurst Community Primary School, Ramsbottom

I Am

A kennings poem

I am a...
Book reader,
Music lover,
Dog petter,
Pizza eater,
Meatball maniac,
Cake baker,
Brother annoyer,
Poem writer,
Friend maker.
This is me.

Ava Carter (10)
Hazlehurst Community Primary School, Ramsbottom

About Me

T all me
H ectic me
I ncredible me
S mart me

I ndependent me
S uper me

M ajestic me
E nergetic me.

Albert Burroughs (10)
Hazlehurst Community Primary School, Ramsbottom

About Me

I am a midfield maestro.
I am a football lover.
I am the proud owner of two pets.
I am the son of two amazing parents.
You will also find me in Tenerife.
This is me.

Oliver Macadam (10)
Hazlehurst Community Primary School, Ramsbottom

It's Me

O melette hater
S peedy runner
C hicken devourer
A stronaut lover
R ad gamer.

This is me.

Oscar Birkett (10)
Hazlehurst Community Primary School, Ramsbottom

Happy To Be Me!

I'm happy to be me,
And you're happy to be you!
You don't need to act like you're somebody else,
Because you have got to be you.
'Cause I'm happy to be me,
And you're happy to be you!
You have got to be you,
You don't need to act like anyone else,
Because you need to be you.
You don't need to be emotional,
'Cause you just have to be you.
I'm happy and you're happy,
So we're all happy to be us.
'Cause I'm happy to be me!
And you're happy to be you!

Ava Winterson (9)
Millbrook Community Primary School, Kirkby

We Are All Different!

Hello, look around! Colourful, right?
Well, imagine if everything was the same...
Now think,
What if every person was the same instead.
Life would be boring.
Now look and think of yourself,
You are... different,
And so is everyone else.
No matter if you are black, white or mixed-race,
Asian or anything else,
You're amazing and always know that,
When you're sad or even happy,
You are great in every way.
You can be great.

Alex McLean (9)
Millbrook Community Primary School, Kirkby

Amelia Alice Messham

I'm Amelia,
I love my family.
I enjoy school,
Entirely.
I was born in 2011.
I got a nephew at seven.
I got a bird at seven.
I got a hamster at eight.
I loved them until they passed,
In a beautiful place called Heaven.
I got a dog at nine,
When I couldn't write on a number line.

Amelia Alice Messham (9)
Millbrook Community Primary School, Kirkby

This Is Me!

My name is Millie,
My mum calls me silly.
I am nine,
And I like to rhyme.
I like school,
It is cool.
I like art,
My friends call me smart.
I am a Scorpio,
I like a good Oreo.
I like Disney,
I also get dizzy,
My name is Millie.

Millie Butler (9)
Millbrook Community Primary School, Kirkby

Motocross

M y name is Michael
I love to ride motocross
C an I win this race?
H ave I got the fastest ride?
A ll are ready at the start
E veryone tries to go as fast as a jet
L ook over there, I am the winner!

Michael Cormode (9)
Millbrook Community Primary School, Kirkby

This Is Me

A haiku

Gaming is my life,
I do it all day and night,
I like the screen bright.

Riley Grimes (9)
Millbrook Community Primary School, Kirkby

This Is Me!

T stands for terrific, meaning wonderful and sensational
H stands for hilarious, meaning amusing and splitting
I stands for intelligent, meaning clever and bright
S stands for sporty, meaning active and energetic

I stands for inspiring, meaning motivating and innovating
S stands for smart, meaning dazzling and outstanding

M stands for marvellous, meaning glorious and superb
E stands for energetic, meaning full of enthusiasm.

This is me!

Zain Muhammed (10)
St Giles' & St George's CE Academy, Newcastle

Lucy Rowlands

L oving and caring
U nique and responsible
C aring and amazing
Y ou shine like the sunshine

R esponsible with everything
O h, I'm not gold but I am a star and I make you smile
W here I've been: Spain and Scotland
L and of Scotland is interesting
A mazing friend I am, I am friendly
N ot like a star, but my heart is made out of gold
D o I like my family? They are loving like me
S unshine warm heart of gold.

Lucy Rowlands (10)
St Giles' & St George's CE Academy, Newcastle

My Family

Dennis is my name,
No day is the same.
I love dinosaurs,
Especially ones on all fours.
I have two siblings,
That do many things.
Sucking his finger is my little brother's hobby,
And my mum waits ages in the lobby.
Delna is my sister,
She has never had a blister.
My dad is a taxi driver,
He is an excellent thriver.
My mum is a nurse,
And she has a tiny purse.

Dennis Jogy (10)
St Giles' & St George's CE Academy, Newcastle

Me!

E arning, I get rewards by earning them. I show
everyone who is kind and pleasant, just like me!
L oving, that's me! Kind and carefree
I ncredible, everybody is amazing, including me!
S trange, we are all weird and crazy, just like me!
E xcellent, we're all brilliant and we're all a bundle
of joy, like me!

Elise Paige Goodwin (9)
St Giles' & St George's CE Academy, Newcastle

All About Me

K is for keep positive
A is for awesome
I is for intelligent and independent

V is for valuable
I is for impressive
R is for reach, you can always reach your goals
G is for greet, always greet your friends
O is for open, tell people you trust about your problems.

Kai Virgo (10)
St Giles' & St George's CE Academy, Newcastle

All About Me

W is for wonderful, so kind and sweet
I is for intelligent, a heavenly treat
L is for lovable, so clever and bright
L is for laughter and musical delight
I is for independent, with a heart so true
A is for awesome, so inspiring
M is for magical, that's what we think you are.

William Burton (9)
St Giles' & St George's CE Academy, Newcastle

Jake Simpson

J is for joyful
A is for awesome
K is for kind
E is for excellent

S is for sensible
I is for incredible
M is for marvellous
P is for perfect
S is for super
O is for obviously, a good friend
N is for nice.

Jake Simpson (9)
St Giles' & St George's CE Academy, Newcastle

Jack

J oker that loves school
A nd strong
C an game
K ind and loves to make friends

A nd doesn't like to watch horror movies
U ltra nice
S hort
T ime is quick
I n my mind, I think boys are better than girls
N ice.

Jack Austin (10)
St Giles' & St George's CE Academy, Newcastle

Daniel

D is for detective, eyes beautiful and green
A is for awesome, that's what we think of you
N is for nice, a heart of gold
I is for intelligent, a brain that's bold
E is for extraordinary, surprising and unusual
L is for lightning, fast and speedy.

Daniel Lambert (9)
St Giles' & St George's CE Academy, Newcastle

The Fabulous Sorocco

S lithery like a snake
O ptimistic and hopeful about the future
R eady for what's coming in life
O utstanding to people and to the world
C reative at making structures
C elebrate my birthday and my career
O utstanding at football and running.

Sorocco Saunders (9)
St Giles' & St George's CE Academy, Newcastle

Scarlett

S is for smart and small Scarlett
C is for caring and cool
A is for artistic and awesome
R is for ravishing red and respectful
L is for loving
E is for enchanting
T is for temper
T is for terrific.

This is me!

Scarlett Twigg (10)
St Giles' & St George's CE Academy, Newcastle

This Is Me

G enerous, kind and loving, day and night
R ecycles litter every day sometimes
A wesome, brightens up people every day
C urious, finds out new things every day
I maginative, wakes up being nice and finds new stuff
E xcitement, full of joy and love.

Gracie Brace (9)
St Giles' & St George's CE Academy, Newcastle

All About Me!

I am friendly and fearless,
So I could be your friend.

I like helping people,
When they are stuck on a question.

I am caring and strong,
I make sure people are okay when they are upset.

I play friendly and kindly with others,
I am kind and loving.

Saskia Roberts (9)
St Giles' & St George's CE Academy, Newcastle

Rebecca

R is for respectful and always polite
E is for energetic and great
B is for brave and as bright as can be
E is for enchanting
C is for caring and calm
C is for cool
A is for amazing and awesome.

This is me!

Rebecca Beesley (11)
St Giles' & St George's CE Academy, Newcastle

All About Me

L is for loving, so sweet and so bright
I is for intelligent, so smart
V is for vibrant, that's very true
V is for violet, so colourful and true
I is for impressed with everything I do
E is for excellent, so bright.

Livvie Davies (9)
St Giles' & St George's CE Academy, Newcastle

Lively Leila

L is for loving, as kind as can be
E is for energetic, as far as you can see
I is for intentional, as nice as can be
L is for loving, a heart full of joy
A is for amazing, as strong as can be.

Leila, the words of life!

Leila Powner (10)
St Giles' & St George's CE Academy, Newcastle

This Is Me!

M is for marvellous
I is for intelligent
L is for like a little star
E is for embarrassing (most of the time)
N is for nice as can be
A is for awesome like a star!

And that is me!

Milena Eardley (9)
St Giles' & St George's CE Academy, Newcastle

About Me!

L is for laughter, so funny and jolly
A is for amazing, as sweet as a lolly
C is for caring like a loving friend
E is for enormously incredible
Y is for youthful, I'm in my younger years.

Lacey Beeley (9)
St Giles' & St George's CE Academy, Newcastle

Masyn

M is for mature, kind and not silly
A is for awesome, that's what we think you are
S is for special, always inspiring
Y is for yourself, just be yourself
N is for nice, as nice as a bee.

Masyn Bowers (10)
St Giles' & St George's CE Academy, Newcastle

Things About Me

A is for awesome because I'm a great friend
M is for magnificent because I'm always right
E is for excellent
L is for loving
I is for incredible
A is for amazing.

Amelia Parton (9)
St Giles' & St George's CE Academy, Newcastle

Eleanor!

E nergetic person
L oving llama
E xcited as always
A mazing me
N ever giving up
O bviously, an amazing friend
R eally cool.

Eleanor, that's me!

Eleanor Reader (9)
St Giles' & St George's CE Academy, Newcastle

Petra

P is for peaceful like a dove
E is for enchanting like a secret garden
T is for terrific, so loud
R is for restful like a person sleeping all day
A is for awesome, so clever.

Petra-Talita Cozea (9)
St Giles' & St George's CE Academy, Newcastle

About Me

C aring and kind
A mazing
M indful and calm
I ncredible and helpful
L ovely and funny
L oving and happy
A ngry and sad.

Yep, that's me!

Camilla Chen (10)
St Giles' & St George's CE Academy, Newcastle

Maram

M indful, so calm and sweet
A dventurous, quite risky but fun!
R esponsible, important and fun
A spirational, always with a goal
M arvellous and majestic, my name is Maram.

Maram Almasri (9)
St Giles' & St George's CE Academy, Newcastle

Lilly

L is for ladybird because it is my favourite
I is for incredible
L is for laughter
L is for loving
Y is for yellow because it is my favourite colour.

Lilly-Mai Copeland (11)
St Giles' & St George's CE Academy, Newcastle

Being Me

K oalas are my favourite animal
E xcited to show my world
R eally cool friend
I nspired to be me
S illy

Keris is my name and this is me.

Keris McGaw (10)
St Giles' & St George's CE Academy, Newcastle

Terrific Tahiya

T is for terrific
A is for awesome
H is for happy
I is for intelligent
Y is for yourself
A is for active.

Tahiya Quayum (10)
St Giles' & St George's CE Academy, Newcastle

Aleah

Hello, I am Aleah and I am 8 years old.
I want to be a baker when I am older.
The things I want to make are cakes,
As well as wedding cakes,
Flapjacks, brownies and cupcakes.
Also, I love to look after my family's children,
And I cook with their children.
My dream has always been to be a baker,
Since I was three.
I started to cook when I was 6 years old.
I am starting to get really good.
Here's a massive tip,
Never give up, always believe, people!
If you don't, you will make me upset,
So follow my tip.

Aleah Walters (8)
The Arbours Primary Academy, Northampton

How To Make A Me Cake

Here's a poem, a poem about me,
And how to make a me cake...

Add a dash of smiles,
A handful of courage,
Crack in some curiosity,
Drop in some purple food dye,
Pour it into the passionate pan,
Cook for five fun minutes,
Once cooked, spread some smart icing,
Sprinkle some sporty sprinkles,
And that's how to make a me cake!
So now cut it with a nice knife,
And plop it onto a positive plate,
Serve for every boy and girl,
To enjoy the lovely me cake.

Lily-Anne Elizabeth Cousins (8)
The Arbours Primary Academy, Northampton

Happy Days

H appiness is the best emotion to have
A lways smile
P layful and fun
P retty butterflies in all colours
Y et, if you cry, just stand up and play

D ads, mums and siblings always help
A nd always trust your family
Y ou be yourself
S adness is the wrong emotion, always be happy.

Ruxanda Basoc (8)
The Arbours Primary Academy, Northampton

Recipe For Me!

You will need:
A pinch of happiness,
A dash of freckles,
Don't be shy, add some of that smartness, dears!
I almost forgot, put some tallness in,
Not too much left now!
Add some brown hair,
And last of all, add some beauty!
To make me!

Maggie Street (8)
The Arbours Primary Academy, Northampton

How To Make Me

To make me, we need lots of happiness,
And then add lots of fun,
Of course, we need a lot of technology,
Let's also add a bit of responsibility,
Don't forget lots of friends,
Also, let's add a bit of kindness,
And you have made me!

Asha Ware-Hussein (8)
The Arbours Primary Academy, Northampton

What I Want To Be When I'm Older

What do I want to be when I'm older?
I want to be a soldier, so I can see all the military gear and stop crime.
Also, I would like to drive the military planes and cars.
I want to be remembered and I want to help the world.

Ollie Howkins (8)
The Arbours Primary Academy, Northampton

Family

F amily is like a big bag of love
A mazing how a family's love can be so splendid
M agnificent family
I love my happy family
L ove families
Y ou would love a happy family.

Freya Cartar (8)
The Arbours Primary Academy, Northampton

How To Make A Rust

You will need:
A spoonful of happiness,
A sprinkle of fun,
A teaspoon of awesomeness,
A handful of smartness,
A bowlful of kindness,
A jugful of friendliness,
A plateful of smiles.

Rust Boss (8)
The Arbours Primary Academy, Northampton

Emily

Hello, my name is Emily,
And I am 8 years old.
I am very happy.
When I grow up, I want to be a nurse at the hospital and help sick people when they're ill.
That's why I want to be a nurse.

Emily Mensah (8)

The Arbours Primary Academy, Northampton

Imran

I mran likes to have some fun
M agnificent work, he does!
R eady to work in a second, just like Flash!
A lready smart like Einstein!
N ot very smart, just very fine.

Imran Islam (8)
The Arbours Primary Academy, Northampton

Esmae

When I grow up, I want to be a teacher.
I want to be a teacher when I grow up,
Because I want to teach children,
And to work with children.
I like playing with my friends at home.

Esmae Kidze (8)
The Arbours Primary Academy, Northampton

Miyah

M iyah likes the colour pink
I love my mum and dad
Y ummy, yummy cake
A lways playing with my cat
H appy is me.

Miyah Simmonds (8)
The Arbours Primary Academy, Northampton

How To Bake A Tasnia

A dash of black, knotty hair,
A tiny pinch of brown eyes,
A handful of laughter,
A sprinkle of happiness,
A pinch of tanned skin.

Tasnia Hadi (8)
The Arbours Primary Academy, Northampton

Young**Writers**
Est. 1991

YOUNG WRITERS INFORMATION

We hope you have enjoyed reading this book – and that you will continue to in the coming years.

If you're the parent or family member of an enthusiastic poet or story writer, do visit our website **www.youngwriters.co.uk/subscribe** and sign up to receive news, competitions, writing challenges and tips, activities and much, much more! There's lots to keep budding writers motivated!

If you would like to order further copies of this book, or any of our other titles, then please give us a call or order via your online account.

Young Writers
Remus House
Coltsfoot Drive
Peterborough
PE2 9BF
(01733) 890066
info@youngwriters.co.uk

Join in the conversation!
Tips, news, giveaways and much more!

YoungWritersUK YoungWritersCW youngwriterscw

Printed in Great Britain
by Amazon

52942871R00126